SCAPEGOAT

SCAPEGOAT

A History of Blaming Other People

CHARLIE CAMPBELL

Duckworth Overlook

First published in the UK and in the US in 2011 by
Duckworth Overlook

LONDON
90-93 Cowcross Street
London EC1M 6BF
info@duckworth-publishers.co.uk
www.ducknet.co.uk

NEW YORK
141 Wooster Street
New York, NY 10012
for bulk or special sales contact sales@overlookny.com

ISBN 978-0-7156-3874-3 (UK)
ISBN 978-1-59020-716-1 (US)

Typeset by Ray Davies
Printed in the UK by
CPI Antony Rowe, Chippenham and Eastbourne

CONTENTS

To my parents

PROLOGUE

It was a dark and stormy night ...

In July 1840 a terrible storm hit St Kilda. The 'island at the end of the world' rises out of the sea 110 miles off the west coast of Scotland. The four islands that form St Kilda boast the highest cliffs in Britain and some of the world's largest colonies of sea birds. This is one of the most unforgiving landscapes on earth and is battered by atrocious weather most of the year. No trees grow here and there is no shelter from the elements. Yet man lived here for over two thousand years, cut off from the outside world for the most part. People on the mainland paid little attention to this furthest outpost of the British Isles, and so the islanders were generally free to live as they chose, only very occasionally disturbed by outsiders.

St Kilda is so isolated that it was often suggested it should be used as a prison, though only one person ever was imprisoned there.[1] And Scotland's turbulent and violent history passed the islanders by – kings came and went, wars were fought, and the Jacobites were defeated at

Culloden. Once, soldiers were sent to investigate rumours that Bonnie Prince Charlie was hiding out there, but they arrived and soon realized that the St Kildans did not even know who the Young Pretender was, let alone support his claim to the throne.

Most Hebridean islands have outlandish legends associated with them, and St Kilda is no exception. Until its evacuation in 1930, it was owned by Macleod of Macleod, chief of the Macleod clan. It is said that ownership had once been contested by both the islands of the Uists and Harris. This dispute was settled by a boat race to St Kilda from the two islands, with the first to lay hand on the shore the winner. As they neared their goal, the Uist men nosed in front of their rivals, but, sensing defeat for his Harris boat, Colla Macleod cut off his left hand and threw it ahead onto the beach, thus becoming the first to claim the island for his master. And ever since then, so the story goes, the Macleod coat of arms has featured a red hand.

The reality of life on St Kilda was no less unusual. The islanders had no leaders and would discuss everything at a daily meeting or parliament. They didn't vote or play any part in affairs on the mainland, nor did they pay any tax. In fact, they had no monetary system and gave rent to

Macleod of Macleod in gull feathers and oil – the sea birds also being their primary source of food. The islanders scaled the cliffs and stacks with incredible agility, dexterously snaring the birds and collecting their eggs. But they were not the hardy seafarers and fishermen you'd expect to inhabit such a place (they were mostly happy for the gannets and puffins to feed on the fish). And so those men out at sea drowned when the great storm of 1840 hit, their boats swamped by the huge waves. A day or two later, the bodies of the dead started to wash up on the shore. Among them was a bedraggled creature, still alive. It was a Great Auk, a large flightless bird that is now extinct, and while no one knew it at the time, this would be the last sighting of one in the British Isles.

The Great Auk was an infrequent visitor to these shores, and the islanders would most likely never have seen anything like it before. Two men netted the bird and took it to the tiny community's church. There it was decided that this was a creature of ill omen who had brought the storm to the island. And so the last British Great Auk was put on trial, charged with being a witch, and found guilty. It was stoned to death on the shoreline where it had been washed up a few days before, by islanders whose own time there was running out.[2]

These days seabirds have St Kilda to themselves.[3] What took place there is the usual story of tragedy striking a small community. Fear, anger and ignorance all combined as the islanders sought an explanation for the calamity that befell them. And, as tends to happen in these situations, an outsider – in this case, the Great Auk – is held responsible for the catastrophe and punished. It is one of mankind's oldest stories, and one of the saddest.

*

Then there is the case of Easter Island, which is even more remote than St Kilda, over two thousand miles off the coast of Chile.

> 'Easter Island punched way above its weight; but it boxed alone, as if in a looking-glass, and we have been able to replay the moves by which it knocked itself out.' (Ronald Wright)

For hundreds of years it was left completely undisturbed by the outside world. The island was divided into 12 or so areas, which fanned outwards from the centre. Different tribes occupied each territory, erecting the giant stone heads (*moai*), for which Easter Island is so famous. These stood on platforms (*ahu*), facing inland, and honoured the islanders' gods and ancestors. Over time, the statues increased in size, suggesting an element of competitiveness, as the tribes strove to outdo each other. The average erected statue weighed 10 tons, but in one quarry there is an unfinished head that weighs in at 270 tons, which surely could never have been moved. In another crater 397 statues have been left. All had been carved out of the rock, then thrown over and abandoned. So why did the statues grow to such an unmanageable size, and why were they toppled?

The answer lies back with the struggle for survival in such a hostile environment. The island used to be heavily wooded; today it is not. From the moment of their arrival in around AD 900, the islanders steadily denuded the place of all its trees. The Easter palm, which once covered the island, was the largest tree of its species, serving many uses – as firewood for cooking and funeral pyres, for thatching and building houses, for making rafts and canoes, and, lastly, for transporting and erecting the giant stone statues.

Over the years, the islanders cleared thousands of trees and moved millions of rocks to create wind breaks and a sunken garden, all in a desperate bid to help certain plants

11

grow. But the deforestation led to soil erosion and the crops duly suffered. Certain animal species gradually disappeared as their habitat was cut back. The land birds were hunted to excess and shellfish overexploited. Meanwhile, the tree clearing continued.

Eventually the day came when the last tree was felled. In *Collapse: How Societies Choose to Fail or Survive*, Jared Diamond asks the famous question: What was going through the mind of the islander the moment he cut down the last tree? (It is estimated that this happened some time between 1400 and 1600.) We shall never know, but from that moment on the islanders fought over every scrap of wood. They had no proper fuel, and stopped cremating bodies, mummifying them instead. They were unable to build canoes and so could not fish. Most importantly, they now were unable to escape from the island. Lastly, they could not build and erect the huge stone statues quite as freely as before. The result of all this was starvation, drastic population decline and, probably, cannibalism. As the severity of their situation became apparent, the islanders turned on each other, and fought and fought.

It is thought that the increase in the size of the statues was linked to the urgency of the islanders' plight, as they turned to their gods for help, building larger and larger figures. But no rescuers came. The statue cult gave way to disenchantment, and the angry islanders started to topple the stone heads they had built to honour their gods once they felt they had been deserted by them. We have to assume that the priests and leaders, who had appointed themselves as go-betweens with the divine, also came to grief as they were shown to be powerless to prevent this disaster.

In his excellent book, *A Short History of Progress*, Ronald Wright observes that the islanders 'carried out for us the experiment of permitting unrestricted population growth, profligate use of resources, destruction of the environment and boundless confidence in their religion to take care of the future. The result was an ecological disaster leading to a population crash.' He asks if we have to repeat the experiment on a larger scale and if the human personality is 'always the same as that of the person who felled the last tree'.[4]

When it comes to taking responsibility for things going wrong, the human personality has always been the same. Today, there is a resistance among the islanders to the idea that their ancestors brought about this calamity, for which several other explanations have been advanced. One modern scientist blames an influx of rats, others diseases brought by passing sailors, while some hold climate change responsible. But the island had survived so many of these phenomena already, that deforestation is left as the most likely explanation. What we don't know is if the islanders thought that technology and hard work would get them through the loss of all their trees. The island was small enough that they should have been aware of the impending disaster. Ultimately Easter Island lost all its trees and with them 90 per cent of its population (and we have to ask ourselves: if Easter Islanders can destroy their environment with such basic tools, how much more are we capable of today?).

This was an example of a pure ecological collapse, a disaster that took place in complete isolation. Uniquely, there were no outsiders to blame – no Jews, no Communists, no Catholics. With no scapegoat around, the island's leaders were unable to direct anger away from themselves, and the blame shifted upwards, through the leaders and priests, and towards the gods.

INTRODUCTION

'Who can we blame?'
Family motto of the Earls of Gresham

In the beginning there was blame. Adam blamed Eve, Eve blamed the serpent, and we've been hard at it ever since. It is our original sin, this refusal to accept responsibility for our actions. It is the reason we were exiled from the Garden of Eden, the reason we work and suffer. But why do we persist in this denial? Well, the blame game's never made any sense – it's just an inbuilt system we have to deflect guilt elsewhere and make it easier to live the unexamined life. But now it's working overtime; nothing is our fault, it seems. We blame as we've always blamed, targeting minority and marginalized groups when things go wrong. But we've found new and unusual ways of doing so too – using pseudo-science and conspiracy theories – and technology makes it easier than ever before to spread these dangerous ideas. Whatever's wrong with us, there might not be a cure, but there's always a culprit.

Marx blamed the capitalist system, Dawkins religion, and Freud thought it all came down to sex.[5] Larkin blamed our parents, Atkins the potato,[6] and Mohamed Al Fayed still says it's all Prince Philip's fault (David Icke agrees with Al Fayed but adds that it's because Prince Philip is a giant extraterrestrial lizard who rules the world). Once we blamed Fate or God, now we blame our genes and our upbringing (with a few stragglers still holding the first two responsible). But blaming our genes is not the same as blaming ourselves. We don't seem much closer to taking full responsibility for our actions and there's always someone to pick on, always a scapegoat.

*

Mankind has achieved so much, made incredible progress in so many fields, and performed extraordinary technological feats. We are taught all about these achievements but rarely about man's stupidity and the ways in which he deceives himself.

'No one ever thinks they're stupid, it's part of their stupidity.' (from *The Wire*, as a detective interrogates a suspect).

This is essentially a book about stupidity, which, as Harlan Ellison stated, is the most common element in the universe along with hydrogen. It's about the particular kind that hits us after disaster, when we single out one person for blame, and hold them responsible for everything. That individual becomes a scapegoat, a lightning conductor[7] for our rage and pain, carrying it away to some other place. Afterwards, we feel that justice has been done, and order restored – until misfortune strikes again. Then the whole furious process of ascertaining responsibility begins once more.

This is a pattern of behaviour that has always been with us, reflecting a deep and universal human need for purification and expiation. Every early society has stories resembling that of the Great Auk, where some unfortunate outsider was saddled with the blame for a disaster beyond the control and understanding of man, and punished or driven out of the community. But these primitive rituals have lingered on in different forms, and they've become increasingly destructive.

In the twenty-first century, we are faced with more choice than ever before – in what we believe, in what we eat, in everything we do. Similarly we have a greater range of things to blame when things go wrong. Whereas our ancestors had to content themselves with the perennial scapegoats – namely women, Jews and certain animals – we are able to apportion blame in ever more imaginative ways for the aspects of our lives and ourselves that disappoint us. The one thing we will not do under any circumstances is accept ourselves as we are. We prefer to find an explanation for why things are not perfect, and these rarely stand up to close scrutiny.

For the wider malaise that affects us all, there are dozens and dozens of conspiracy theories, all rooted in the idea that some shadowy force is to blame – whether it be the Freemasons, the Illuminati or giant lizards; Communists, Jews or Catholics. For our individual problems, we have endless possible explanations; whole industries have sprung up to provide more authoritative ones. Blame has gradually become a product, to be bought and sold like any other. And those who trade in it have tended to become extraordinarily successful.[8]

The relationship between the blamer and the blamed is a complex one. Really, the opposite of the prince is not the pauper, it is the scapegoat. As we will see later, the ruler creates the scapegoat so he doesn't share his fate. We like to have our hate figures, just as we like to have leaders (though we tend to loathe them both equally). They are inextricably linked, reverse sides of a coin, one the shadow of the other – much in the way God and the Devil are in Christianity. The basic rule is as follows: the more a leader promises, the more he or she will subsequently have to apportion blame. Once we thought our kings were divine and therefore infallible, that disaster had to be the fault of another. These days we elect our leaders on the back of unrealistic promises which we choose to believe. They fail in these and we replace our leaders rather than overhaul the system, which resists change. And so the cycle of promise and blame begins all over again.

Think of William Golding's *Lord of the Flies*, a book that has been required reading for most teenagers since its publication in the 1950s. A group of small children is stranded on a desert island after a plane crash. In the absence of adults and established order, events descend into chaos quickly, in the midst of which leaders and victims emerge. Ralph is chosen as the boy to lead the children over Jack, the head of the choir. Meanwhile, Piggy emerges as the most obvious target for the boys' cruelty – fat and bespectacled, he invites persecution. But as the novel progresses, Ralph falls from grace as he tries to protect Piggy from the others. Jack gradually replaces Ralph, having realized and exploited the importance of Piggy's role. And so the original leader and the scapegoat both find themselves outsiders, fighting for their survival, as Jack and the choir scour the island for them. This all shows how the leader and the scapegoat both exist on the margins of a society.

This relationship is most visible in politics. Such is the intensity of the media spotlight these days that all potential crises need to be dealt with in a way that satisfies the watching public. That public is most easily appeased by the creation of a scapegoat. As always, the more serious the crisis, the more important the fall guy. Think of politicians stepping down 'to spend time with their family'. Chancellor of the Exchequer Norman Lamont was held responsible for Black Wednesday in 1992, when sterling was ignominiously ejected from the ERM. As a result he was gradually marginalized, before being sacked the following year. Lord Carrington stepped down after the Argentine invasion of the Falklands in 1982. As Foreign Secretary, he wasn't personally at fault for his department's failure to foresee Galtieri's actions, but he took responsibility for the mistakes and complacency of the Foreign Office, under the doctrine of ministerial responsibility.[9]

Throughout history, it is only in the most exceptional of circumstances that a ruler will admit culpability. And quite often that is what makes the leader exceptional – a willingness to admit fallibility and learn from it. After losing half his troops at the battle of Gettysburg in 1863, Civil War General Robert E. Lee declared, 'All of this has been my fault. I asked more of my men than should have been asked of them.' In the same way, in the days before the Normandy invasion, General Eisenhower prepared a short speech accepting all blame in the event of failure. A readiness to admit to mistakes may not win the battle, but it can help win the war.

But in today's political culture of spin, modern leaders are less ready than ever to admit fallibility. The phrase 'mistakes were made ...' has entered the political lexicon, as the most passive and detached way of acknowledging error, rather than responsibility. It has been a particular favourite of twentieth-century American politicians, from Nixon and Kissinger to Reagan and Clinton. These three words were used repeatedly by Republicans in the aftermath of the Iraq war.

This brings us to the most dangerous use of scapegoats – the blaming of certain individuals to give governments the freedom to act in certain ways. This is an age-old strategy, and, most recently, Saddam Hussein, Osama bin Laden and Abu Musab al-Zarqawi were all similarly demonized. The latter was used to prove a non-existent link between the first two, giving the American public the sense of a greater threat against them than in fact existed, and justifying the use of military force in Iraq. As one can see, the urge to blame is sometimes incited in us, and this form of demonization has been employed for centuries.

But let us look outside politics, for a moment, at the instances of scapegoating that happen in other hierarchies. The most extreme examples occur after a terrible event such as the murder of a child. While the police search for the perpetrator, the media conduct a frenzied witch-hunt, looking to hold someone else accountable also. Public anger is not focused solely on the wrongdoer; more explanation is needed. We like to believe that there is a system in place to protect us from evil such as this. And so, someone in authority must be held responsible, usually a social worker. The choice of scapegoat may seem entirely random but that is not the case – they will be chosen because they hold a position of responsibility and yet are not utterly indispensable. The social worker can be an object of distrust because he does a job that the public doesn't fully understand, and as a result does not seem as irreplaceable or admirable as, say, a policeman is.

A military defeat will usually produce a scapegoat or

two. The Charge of the Light Brigade saw blame pinned on Lord Lucan and Captain Nolan, rather than Lord Raglan, who issued the original order that was both unclear (in designating which guns should be attacked) and contrary to standard military practice at the time (launching a cavalry attack against enemy guns and infantry, without support). At sea, Admiral Byng was blamed unfairly for the loss of Minorca in the Seven Years' War and executed by firing squad, leading Voltaire to write that sometimes an admiral should be shot *'pour encourager les autres'*. And an improbable number of Special Forces missions have come unstuck after their chance discovery by a boy and his herd of goats. There's always a goat to account for things having gone wrong.

In 2007, the world entered the worst economic crisis since the Great Depression of the 1930s. It had been caused by the bursting of the American housing bubble, leading to the spectacular collapse of Lehman Brothers in September 2008. The fallout was global, and saw plenty of scapegoats targeted – from rich bankers and their bonuses, to short-selling hedge fund managers thought to have profited from the downturn, and chief executives whose self-interested, rash decisions led to this calamity. How much easier it is to attribute responsibility to them, rather than face the truth of our own involvement. The notion of collective responsibility is one that we prefer not to engage with. Only those who were financially very prudent can exempt themselves from blame. The rest of us were happy to run up more debt than could be sustained for long by a banking system that depends, like so much of institutional life and commerce, on public confidence. This debt was parceled up and reshaped in a way that, for a while, concealed its origins. But ultimately it choked the system. And we shrieked at the likes of Fred Goodwin, chief executive of Royal Bank of Scotland, blaming him for what we had lost. He was criticized for excessive spending and labelled 'the world's worst banker' after RBS posted an annual loss of £24.1bn, the largest in UK corporate history. As details of his pension emerged, his house was vandalized, as the public sought redress.

As I write, the venues for the 2018 and 2022 football World Cups are being decided (corruptly, as it turns out), and we can be sure those tournaments will produce as many villains as they do heroes. It is ironic that *team* sports should produce so many fall guys – so many individuals held responsible for an entire team's defeat. Think of David Beckham after the World Cup in 1998. These days he may be a national icon, with the shameful public reaction to his sending off against Argentina forgotten; back then effigies of him were burned publicly across the country. But this was harmless enough compared to the fate of Andrés Escobar. The Colombian defender scored the own goal that put his country out of the 1994 World Cup. He was shot dead on his return to his homeland – it is thought, on the orders of drugs lords who had sustained large gambling losses as a result of his mistake. But, in football, even the penalty shoot-out is structured to put the blame for defeat on one or two players. And referees are invariably blamed by managers and supporters for a team's defeat.

The concept of a sporting scapegoat is perfectly illustrated by the average career of a football manager in the English Premiership. A Premiership club is a reasonably simple organization – you have the board who run the club, and you have the team who do the ball-kicking bit. The biggest, most financially successful clubs are able to afford a few truly world-class players who make them unstoppable on a good day. Yet some teams are more successful than others despite operating within similar parameters. That comes down to the ability of a manager to motivate his players and make them play as a team. Those clubs who aren't doing well are faced with a decision – of making a change. Most managers in the

Premiership have proved themselves elsewhere and it might well be the players who are letting him down. But it will almost always be the manager who is replaced (bureaucrats never sack themselves and the players are numerous and all tied to long-term deals). Suddenly a fresh wind blows through the club and results often improve. The manager is the scapegoat who departs, taking the sense of defeat and negativity with him. Yet everyone in the football world knows that it is not his fault. And this is why he is highly paid and will walk into another job straight afterwards.

All of this shows that this instinct to blame is fundamental to our being. We cannot help it, but we can be made aware of it, and so be in a position to resist it. I want this to be a book that will make people think more about the issue of blame and responsibility. We all have our own personal stories of disaster and in each there will often have been at least one person acting as our own scapegoat, however unconsciously we may have cast them as such. And sometimes we may have been scapegoated ourselves. Just as we like to take things to pieces to see how they work when we're children, we like to do the same as adults, after crises. Look at the time and money spent on enquiries following tragedies such as Hillsborough,

Bloody Sunday, even the death of Princess Diana. But these situations rarely make perfect sense.

Some of the stories in this book will seem so ludicrous and backward that they may amuse rather than shock. And there is much comedy to be found here, but it is balanced by tragedy. The persecution of witches has often been played for laughs by subsequent generations, and there is something inherently absurd about it, certainly the practice of 'swimming' suspected witches – if they float they're guilty, if they drown they were probably innocent. But what could be more hateful than a society purging itself of its weakest and least economically valuable members in a time of crisis? There is much that just evokes horror here.

Much of this will seem obvious – in that burning women and blaming Jews for the Black Death are both clearly wrong, blatantly so. But our forebears nonetheless did these things and we forget our own capacity for similar crimes at our peril. It has been said that there is nothing more unfair than judging men, women and societies of the past by the values of the present. In many ways that's true, but we should remind ourselves of these follies. To guard against any complacency of our own, however, we should ask which of our modern-day delusions future generations might hold up as being every bit as lunatic. We may like to think, after reading about the sacrifice of human scapegoats, that we have moved on from such cruel practices, but we haven't – only the methods have changed. Underneath, we are still the same primitive beings.

No short history can be comprehensive, and there will be omissions – many intentional, others less so. And some may disagree with my conclusions, thinking that a given person really *was* to blame. They could be right. What I really want to do is to draw attention to our capacity to blame, and the danger of listening to that insidious inner voice when emotions are running high in the aftermath of disaster. As already mentioned, I want to show how the opposite of the prince is not the pauper, but the scapegoat – he or she who takes the fall when things turn bad, as opposed to leaders who have taken credit throughout history when things have gone well, regardless of the extent of their own involvement.

This is not meant to be revisionist history, revisionist history being the deliberate portrayal of an alternative view of the past. Primary sources have always offered contradictory views. Some think that history is always written by the victors, and that the identities of the hero and the villain are determined accordingly. Most history does indeed focus on the deeds of great men rather than social ones which concentrate on the lives of the overlooked masses. In this book I hope to shine a light on those who were accused of directing the course of history (onto the rocks most of the time), when in fact they didn't. Really they were marginal figures who were taken by their enemies and placed at the centre of things, with powers that they never had attributed to them.

So, what is the importance of this subject and how is this relevant to us now? The reader will bear witness to thousands of years of the use and abuse of scapegoats. Scapegoating is with us now in so many different guises. Many of the examples in this book will immediately call to mind their modern counterparts. We may have made enormous strides in other fields but human nature has remained pretty constant. We still crave simple explanations for complex happenings. And we cannot help but hold each other responsible when things go wrong. We take false comfort in blaming others and in an age of technology where spreading these ideas has never been easier, it is perhaps an opportune time to take stock.

THE WORD 'SCAPEGOAT'

'They were trying to use me as an escape goat.'
Jade Goody on *Big Brother*

The word 'scapegoat' was first used by William Tyndale, the translator of the Bible, in his 1530 edition.[10] He coined it to describe a ritual from the Jewish Day of Atonement in Leviticus. In this two goats are sacrificed. The first is sacrificed to Yahweh, so that he might pardon Israel. This goat is a 'sin offering' and its sacrifice is an act of atonement by the people. Its remains are burned outside the community. The second goat is dedicated to Azazel, a god of the underworld. It is saddled with 'all the iniquities of the children of Israel, and all their transgressions in all their sins' by the high priest of Yahweh, and driven into the wilderness. The goat is led outside the village boundaries and left there. It cuts a sorrowful figure – as Holman Hunt showed in his painting 'The Scapegoat' – abandoned in a desolate landscape, with red tassels tied to its horns. When these have been bleached white by the sun, the sins are deemed to have been expiated. The congregation's sense of guilt is passed on and expelled from the community. It stays in the wilderness, which could be a special and powerful place for a shaman or prophet. But the desert, when entered unwillingly, is only a curse. And that is how Holman Hunt shows it.

Tyndale, it is interesting to note, met with a fate even worse than the goat's. He had sought to translate the Bible into English, and in doing so, to make scripture available to everyone through the new technology of printing with movable type.[11] But this brought him into conflict with the Church at a time when translating the Bible from the Vulgate's fourth-century Latin was heresy. As it was, very few could read God's word, and congregations were dependent on their priests to decode scripture for them. Tyndale saw the clergy as too stupid, corrupt and dissolute to be entrusted with the salvation of others. He believed that only direct exposure to the word of God could bring about change, removing the Church as the link to the divine.

The Church's power was not founded on scripture; there is no mention in the Bible of the pope, nor does it set up any hierarchy for man to rule over man. But the clergy protected themselves from change by locking scripture behind this barrier of language. They justified this ban on translating the Bible by saying that laymen were too taken up with worldly affairs to keep the pure, quiet mind that was necessary for reading scripture. Tyndale hit back, saying, 'This weapon strikes themselves, for who is so tangled with worldly matters as the prelates.' He predicted that he would one day make it possible for a ploughboy to know more scripture than a scholar. His translation also allowed women to read the Bible, something that again upset traditionalists greatly.[12]

So, when Tyndale approached the Bishop of London seeking patronage for his translation, he did not meet with approval. The clergy were then the city's largest property owners and employers too. They effectively controlled the printing presses, and Tyndale was forced to travel to the Continent to find someone who would risk publishing his translation. His copies were smuggled into England and distributed covertly – and pirated by others. There was a lot of money to be made from this trade in illegal Bibles, though Tyndale sought none of it, living extremely modestly and relying on the patronage of merchants. Sixteen thousand copies of Tyndale's Bible were distributed in a country with a population of two and a half million, many of whom were illiterate (per capita, the equivalent of 326,400 copies today). It is a staggering number, though only a couple of copies survive today. Ownership of one was an act of heresy; not that this applied to the Church. The Bishop of London arranged for many copies to be bought, so they could be burned in public view. Even the most traditionally-minded baulked at this inconsistent approach to the written word of God.

Tyndale not only challenged the Church by allowing everyone to read scripture, he went one step further. His translation had one crucial difference from the Vulgate. He translated the Greek word 'εκκλησια' as 'congregation' rather than 'church', so stripping the latter of their authority. He denied the Church's claim to have inherited leadership of the faith from St. Peter. Tyndale was steadily gathering enemies, most notably Thomas More, who became fixated with his heresy and wrote longingly of burning him. Ironically, Tyndale had translated passages in the Bible that would one day be used to condemn him: 'And the fyre shall trye every man's worke, what it is.'[13] More and Tyndale wrote hundreds of thousands of words, railing endlessly against each other. Tynale was as elegant and expressive as ever, More less so (wearing a hair shirt and whipping oneself does not hone one's writing style). He accused Tyndale of fomenting unrest, going as far as to blame him for the Peasants' War in Germany (which had claimed over 70,000 lives), and describing him as a hell-hound. Tyndale was equally outspoken, writing of the Church: 'The parson sheareth, the vicar shaveth, the parish priest polleth, the friar scrapeth, and the pardoner pareth. We lack but a butcher to pull off the skin.'

Unsurprisingly, Tyndale was condemned as a heretic and blamed for the religious turmoil that was sweeping Europe. In some ways then, he was almost a scapegoat, a man on whom could be placed responsibility for the religious trauma that was happening. He was demonized and declared a heretic when in truth he represented traditional Christian values far more than the Church with whom he found himself in conflict. Really he was a symptom of the ills that organized religion was undergoing. The Church was arrogant and out of touch with the common man. Henry VIII put his sexual desire ahead of his kingly duty. Luther was leading a revolt against an upheaval of tradition on the Continent. But it was easier to pick on an outsider and hold him responsible.

Having spent many years lying low in Europe, Tyndale was eventually betrayed and captured in Antwerp in 1535. He was subjected to a degrading ritual in which he was stripped of his priestly dignity before being thrown into a cell. Through all of this, he impressed his gaolers with his decency and calm. One said that if he 'were not a good Christian man, they could not tell whom they might take to be one.' But his few supporters were unable to delay his undoing, and the following year he was strangled and burned at the stake. He left an enormous legacy, and his translation lives on in the King James Version of the Bible – 84 per cent of the New Testament is largely his work, as is 76 per cent of the Old Testament. And he opened the way for others; four translations of the Bible were published in the four years after his death, one of them being the official English version. The Christian faith owes much to Tyndale, as much as it does to any church leader. It is often the undoubted beauty of his writing that makes passages of the Bible so memorable, rather than the actual message the scripture carries. He and Shakespeare are two of the dominant figures in the English canon, and the word 'scapegoat' was just one of his many gifts to us.

THE RITUAL SCAPEGOAT

Definition of a scapegoat: *'Any material object, animal,
bird or person on whom the bad luck, diseases, misfortunes
and sins of an individual or group are symbolically placed,
and which is then turned loose, driven off with stones, cast
into a river or the sea, etc, in the belief that it takes away
with it all the evils placed upon it.'*

Funk and Wagnall's Standard Dictionary
of Folklore, Mythology and Legend

The ritual of the scapegoat goes back right to the beginning
of mankind. Every early culture had ceremonies in which
they removed sin from the community. These varied
greatly, but one thing was constant – the idea that sin was a
definite entity that could be transferred from being to being,
or object, and that wrongdoing could be washed away. As
a species, we're obsessed by purity. All belief systems are
not just devices we use to make sense of the world, they
allow us to hope that we can return to a state of innocence.

The ancients believed that spirits surrounded us,

residing in plants, rocks and animals. The Romans had their sacred groves, while the Arabs thought the desert to be populated by the jinn. A widespread confusion between the physical and the mental led to a firm belief in the transmission of evil. In *The Golden Bough* Sir James Frazer describes many examples of this from all over the world. In the East Indian Islands, the inhabitants thought a malign spirit could be channeled into leaves which were held against the patient, then thrown away. In China, kites were used to spirit sickness away; in the Aleutian Islands it was weeds. In Indonesia, villagers built little boats to carry away their demons. In India they buried their sins in a jar, which any unwary passer-by could stumble upon, like an unwitting Pandora (there was little concern with what subsequently happened to the expelled evil). Iroquois Indians painted and decorated their oldest friends, before strangling them. In the Himalayas dogs were stoned to death to expiate sin; in Scotland the dogs merely got chased. In India and Egypt cows were the animal of choice. And so on. All of this is a logical step towards transferring evil to another human.

Human scapegoats came to be used more frequently in time. The animals that were sacrificed as scapegoats were usually of high value, but their human counterparts tended to be society's marginal figures – criminals or the disabled. Sometimes they could be priests, whose holy status protected them from this contact with evil. Or they could be actors who were paid for their duties and the risks they took on. These scapegoats were used either as part of a regular ceremony or in the aftermath of disaster. Some cultures had ceremonies in which the scapegoat was dressed in fine robes and led through the crowds as they cast their sins upon him. He would then be driven out of the village and stoned, or thrown into a river or off a cliff, thus carrying away all the people's ills.

There are countless instances of such rituals. Babylon's most important religious celebration was that of *Akitu*, celebrating the arrival of the new year (in our month of April). In this, the king was deposed and stripped of his insignia of office. He was then restored to his throne with a ritual which involved slapping him in the face until he wept. Afterwards a human scapegoat, usually a condemned criminal, was paraded through the streets, then thrown out of the city and killed, to signal the beginning of the new year. In Albania sacred slaves were kept in the Temple of the Moon. One who showed exceptional signs of inspiration and insanity was chained up for a year, anointed with oils, then speared to death.

The sins of the people were then transferred to his corpse and the future foretold from the way it had fallen. In Tibet a man with his face painted half white and half black was proclaimed the King of Years. He sat in the market place every day while passers-by cast their sins onto him. Then he was driven out of the city to spend the next 12 months living in a cave. If he survived, he returned the next year and took on the same role. The Hebrews used scapegoats to deal with minor sins, though more serious transgressions – known as abominable sins – could not be dealt with like this; these included sodomy and having sex with one's wife and mother-in-law at the same time.

In Ancient Greece the scapegoat was known as the *pharmakos* and, as elsewhere, he performed a key role in society, cleansing it of a sense of wrongdoing after disaster.[14] In Athens a number of outcasts were fed and housed at the city's expense. If disaster struck, two of them were sacrificed, one on behalf of the men, one for the women. The scapegoats were dressed in robes and were led around the city while prayers were uttered for the city's sins to fall on them. Then they were taken outside the city walls and stoned to death. Similar rituals happened elsewhere in Greece, involving others on the margins of society. The Leucadians threw a criminal into the sea each year, tying birds and feathers to him, as a sacrifice to Apollo. The Greeks of Asia Minor used dwarves and the deformed as their scapegoats. These unfortunates were fed, beaten ritually on the genitals to the sound of flute music, then burned to death. In the annual harvest festival of Thargelia two scapegoats were sacrificed, usually the ugliest men who could be found. They were led around with strings of figs hanging from their necks, before undergoing the usual genital-whipping, stoning and burning.

Mary Renault's novel *The Praise Singer* (1978) depicts a scene where the citizens of Ephesos select the *pharmakos*, faced with the barbarian army of Medes outside their walls. They chose a swindler and paraded him naked through the town.

They stripped him, and put the ritual offering-cakes in his hands, having to tie them there because he shook so, and led him out to the gate. There they beat him as the rite prescribes, on his tenderest parts till he screamed aloud. Then everyone fell on him as they chose, to purge their offences which he carried for them, and drove him along with sticks and cudgels till

he fell. I don't know if he was dead when they came
to throw him on the bonfire.

The Romans were a little more civilized than their neighbours
but had similar purification rituals. Every March a man
dressed in skins and representing Old Mars was led through
the streets of Rome. He was then beaten with white rods and
driven out of the city as a way of ushering out the old year and
welcoming in the new, in the hope of a good harvest. The
Romans also had the festival of Saturnalia, which was a period
of general licence. Masters would serve their slaves and all
manner of things were permitted, from excessive drinking
and dancing to sex. Afterwards one individual would be
punished, lifting guilt from the others.

The ancients believed that human sin could be purged
through rituals. They developed them to appease the gods,
who watched over everything. The rituals were a way of
sending a message to the heavens to atone for the sins of a
community and avert punishment. In this climate of utter
ignorance of how natural events happened it was believed
that plagues, famines and the like were a divine
judgement. And so these ceremonies for removing sin and
sickness were usually conducted at times of severe
seasonal change when mortality rose – at the beginning or

end of winter or during the monsoon. These rituals allayed the people's fear of infertility, both that relating to childbirth and the harvest.

This method of removing sin has evolved over the centuries. What was once an ancient expiatory ritual, aimed at deflecting the wrath of the gods and cleansing a society, has mutated into a method by which rulers can channel the anger of their subjects away from themselves and onto some poor unfortunate. Over time the term scapegoat has come to refer to any group or individual on whom falls the outpouring of anger and blame following disaster. There are essentially two types of modern or post-ritual scapegoats: those created unconsciously, as an expression of our rage and incomprehension, in whose guilt everyone believes; and those created as a conscious act, by those seeking to deflect blame away from themselves. The unconscious ones came first, and existed the moment disaster struck. But in time it became a conscious process – as conscious as the ancient rituals, but lacking the sense of theatre and the acknowledgement that the victim was just that, a victim.

The 'sin-eater' is perhaps the only continuation of these ancient rituals. In the Middle Ages a practice emerged for the transferring of the sins of the dead. At funerals, sin-eaters were paid to take on the sins of those who had recently died to aid their progression to heaven and save them from purgatory. They sat next to the corpse, and food and drink were passed over it to them. By eating and drinking it, they appropriated the sins of the deceased. Understandably, it was not a sought-after job, and the rest of the time sin-eaters were treated no better than lepers. The practice was widespread in Britain, particularly in Wales and the Hebrides, and instances of it were recorded as late as the nineteenth century. The last known sin-eater, Richard Munslow, died in 1906. He was a Shropshire farmer, and from all accounts was not the unfortunate figure normally associated with the role.

Brewer records the following: 'In Carmarthenshire the sin-eater used to rest a plate of salt on the breast of the deceased and place a piece of bread on the salt. After saying an incantation over the bread it was consumed by the sin-eater and with it he ate the sins of the dead.'

The main difference between this role and that of the scapegoat is that the sin-eater performed his duties on behalf of the dead, and he was always permitted to live afterwards, if not with comfort and respect. Also, he would have been paid for his services.

Scapegoating is suddenly no longer a ritual act, but a

behavioural pattern; no longer a way of safeguarding a community, but instead one that protects one or two people. Every time there is a catastrophic event the majority finds a minority to blame. Sometimes it happens almost organically, at others the mob is steered towards its victim by the king.

THE KING AND THE SCAPEGOAT

'Don't touch me, I'm special.'
Johnny Rotten, on being tapped on the
shoulder in a pub in Ireland

Before we examine the scapegoat further, let us look quickly at those who rule us. Count Axel Oxenstierna, the Chancellor of Sweden during the Thirty Years' War, famously wrote, 'Know, my son, with how little wisdom the world is governed.' Obviously he was right, but why should this be so? How is it that our leaders and bureaucrats fail us so much and so often? Are our structures of government innately flawed? In a healthy hierarchy blame should flow upwards (with it being passed down in a corrupt one). But how often does this happen? Robert Anton Wilson wrote of the Howard Hughes syndrome, where everybody lies to the man in power, some to gain favour, others to escape punishment. The result is that the person at the top feeds on 'flattering and deceptive garbage' and gets a very warped view of how things really stand. Few people in that situation are likely to accept anything other than praise. And, after all, we should remember that in a hierarchy everyone knows what to do, except for the leader. He is alone in having to decide what to do.

A rival explanation for why things always go wrong can be found in that wonderful study of incompetence, *The Peter Principle*. Its author, Raymond Hull, noted that, 'with few exceptions, men bungle their affairs,' and maintained that in every hierarchy we rise to the level above that at which we are competent, and there we stay. Most achievements are down to those who have yet to reach their level of incompetence. But is there a way of breaking this, of promoting people to the right level? After all, modern rulers rely on those beneath them more than ever. They have to devote themselves to so many issues, which they will rarely be able to understand fully, rarely having enough time to think about them properly. So they have to rely excessively on the bureaucracy that supports them, which will always perpetuate itself.

The Stoics maintained that reason was the 'thinking fire' that steered world events, and the ruler of a state was 'the servant of divine reason [appointed] to maintain order on earth.'[15] Plato believed in the idea of philosopher-kings, who would be educated in such a way that they would rule the world with perfect wisdom. But his scheme of breeding great rulers was never brought to fruition. The mandarins of China tried something similar, putting potential administrators through years of study. The Turks attempted the same in the Ottoman Empire, taking Christian children from their homes and training them for leadership. And some might add to this the British establishment's system of public schools, which for years produced the administrators of one of the most successful empires in history, sending them to be educated away from their parents at a young age, stunting somewhat their ability for empathy and understanding of others (particularly the native people of the Empire). But how do you bring up someone for such a rarified role as that of leadership? And, if we don't consciously train and create rulers, how do they reach their position? For answers, we have to look at ourselves.

Man is essentially a meaning-seeking creature. Our desire for significance in this life is every bit as strong as our need for food and shelter. Essentially we are incapable of accepting that much of life is inexplicable. And so we use myth, art and religion as devices to explain and cope with reality. Through them, we tell stories to dispel this

49

frightening notion that the universe is a violent and senseless place where anything can and will happen to us. We listen most carefully to those who tell us that this isn't actually the case, to those who can offer an explanation. And this all too often turns into blame. Blame tells the most comforting story, one in which there is a villain who seeks to thwart us, the heroes, at every turn. We are led to believe that if the villain is removed, all will be well.

For most of our time on earth we have lived close to hunger; the fear of famine has never been far away. It was only when we moved away from a hunter-gatherer's existence and towards an organized system of agriculture that a food surplus was created. This changed everything, allowing a degree of leisure for some. No longer did each man have to labour every day to feed himself and his family. Some were able to take on roles other than those of hunter and farmer. The stockpiling of food created kings, priests and bureaucrats (and art, in case it sounds only like a bad thing). The first two claimed to be intermediaries to the gods who could intercede on man's behalf, or even claimed divine status themselves. They offered explanations for and protection from the turbulence of existence. In return for these services, they received a higher standard of living. Their negotiations with the divine tended to result in the acquisition of power and vast tracts of land for themselves. It is worth pointing out that religion was not their creation; this is a manifestation of our true nature which is not secular, but they exploited it to the full. They ensured through feudal systems that the masses had no rights in this world, while through religion they taught them that they had every right in the next. This was the perfect way for the élite to protect their power, and so it has continued for centuries.

Early Sumerian theology held that man was created to relieve the gods of the burden of work. And for thousands of years since then, we have worked. Mankind has been largely submissive, the vast majority sacrificing themselves so that a small minority could live in comfort. They did this because they had been given great promises of protection against the unknown. But there were risks involved in this. The earliest communities had leaders who were semi-divine, and who nominally ruled the community as kings. Often they represented the god of vegetable fertility and so were rarely allowed to die a natural death. Instead, to spare them the ravages of old age, and so they could be resurrected in a stronger form, they were ritually killed. Understandably, as time went on, the more resourceful leaders tried to avoid this fate and introduced the idea of death by proxy. A convicted criminal might be chosen to die in the king's stead, or one of the king's children might take his place – one Swedish ruler sacrificed eight of his offspring.

So royalty could be a considerable burden. Not only could a king face ritual murder at the first sign of a grey hair but he was held responsible for all natural calamities. In Copan in AD 850, the king failed to deliver on his promises of rain and prosperity and so his people turned on him, blaming him for their troubles, and burned down his palace. As happened much later on Easter Island, the people's anger flowed upwards towards their leader. There were many other similar occurrences, as rulers sought to deflect blame, and so the scapegoat came into being. Ritual seasonal ceremonies were slowly superseded by human scapegoats.

As we can see, the king and the scapegoat exist at opposing ends of society, but are connected on a fundamental level. The king creates the scapegoat lest he share his fate, but their roles are not always entirely separate. The king can become the scapegoat, whereas the reverse cannot happen. One is basically powerless, the other all-powerful. And yet the underdog is credited with as much power as the king, being seen as able to cause catastrophe at will. By attributing such power to their enemies, rulers effectively strengthen themselves. They create a fear of their enemies and use this to grant themselves further power. They are able to bypass normal conventions of law and justice, claiming that their enemies are so formidable and their acts so evil as to require special measures. Normal rules cannot apply. This has gone on throughout history. Just as witchcraft was declared *crimen exceptum* by the Catholic Church in the fifteenth century, so George W. Bush declared war on terror post-9/11 and ignored much of the Geneva Convention when dealing with suspected al-Qaeda terrorists. In both cases a vast, meticulously organized conspiracy was alleged, and a more threatening enemy created.

Leaders have always demonized their enemies, making them out to be evil and malign and accusing them of every unnatural practice and sin. This has the effect of dehumanizing them, creating the idea that they are a lower form of life, that they actually deserve their terrible treatment and that persecuting them is the right thing to do. Scapegoats are always demonized, but with that extra ingredient of blame that makes the persecution that much harsher, and gives it an illusion of rationality, even virtue. The king or leader can create a scapegoat for when things go wrong, perhaps in the form of an enemy outside his people's borders working tirelessly against them, as in the Soviet Union, when Stalin blamed everything on Trotsky. Equally, the king could hold a sinister 'enemy within' responsible for his country's woes, as happened with the persecution of the Jews, and with the witch craze of the Middle Ages.

There is another type of scapegoat employed by the king – a figure very close to him who would take the blame in certain situations. The first occurrence of this would be the whipping boy. At a time when kings were still thought to have divine status it was not believed right to punish the prince or king should they transgress in any way when young. Yet it was considered important for some punishment to be meted out to show them that they had done wrong. So a courtier of around the young prince's age would be punished in his stead. These stand-ins would be known as whipping boys. They were usually well-born and educated with their master from birth, often becoming friends and forming a strong bond. The prince would have few other playmates, so this relationship was an important one, and it was thought that to see his companion punished in his place would upset the prince and make him less likely to stray afterwards.

Several English kings had whipping boys in their youth and quite often they would ennoble them for their services later on. Charles I's whipping boy started life as plain William Murray but became the Earl of Dysart and lived in Ham House for a good deal of his life. One could argue that he fared better than his ill-fated master. It could also be argued that our current system of ennoblement in exchange for donations to political parties may be corrupt, although it represents progress from a system based on spanking. Other monarchies used these whipping boys too. When Henry IV of France became a Catholic in 1593, he sent two of his ambassadors, D'Ossat and Du Perron, to Rome to suffer any punishment the pope felt he should receive. Clement VIII had them beaten on the steps of St. Peter's as they sang the *Miserere*. They were eventually made cardinals.

After the whipping boy came the minister-favourite, who would perform much the same role for the king at a later stage in life, though with more politics and less spanking (if you discount Edward II and Piers Gaveston, who did both).[16] The minister-favourite was a dominant figure at court, particularly in the seventeenth century, but he existed before that, and continues to do so. He was a courtier whose closeness to the king created enormous tension throughout the rest of the court. He would be blamed for any unpopular decisions taken by the king, and there was no way of removing him, short of assassination or the monarch tiring of him (though the English tried using impeachment to effect this removal). These favourites existed outside the established channels of power and influence, relying on intimacy with the ruler (which could be sexual, as between Catherine the Great and Potemkin) to maintain their position. They served in a private capacity, with no official status, and so were not subject to the authority of others. Really, they were Merlin-like figures, keeping to the shadows, and blamed for bewitching the ruler. They acted as 'the negative identity of a king who could do no wrong; he was a buffer, a lightning conductor, or at worst a burning-glass interposed between king and people at a time when a moral consensus for government policy could not be relied upon.'[17]

It used to be the aim of every courtier to become the king's favourite. Baldassare Castiglione wrote that, 'The goal of the perfect courtier' was to gain 'the love of his master in such a complete way as to become his favourite.' But others felt that that betokened excessive ambition. The Jesuit Juan de Mariana believed that for a king to be surrounded by fawning courtiers would lead to tyranny, and was therefore the worst thing.

The religious conflict in Europe of the years 1550–1650 meant that it was extremely useful for a ruler to have a minister-favourite to draw the sting from the attacks of both the religious extremists and the staunch traditionalists, it being impossible to keep both sides happy. The ruler could present himself as the bluff, well-meaning monarch, while the courtier could practise *realpolitik* openly. The proof of the success of this system is how these courtiers were almost universally vilified in the place of their masters. Alleging that a king had fallen victim to the sorcery of another and that that influence was colouring his decisions was really the only way of criticizing a ruler without challenging his authority. The people could accept the omnipotence of a king, but not that of a favoured courtier.

The latter have modern equivalents. These include Nancy Reagan (accused of influencing her husband with her belief in astrology), Martin Bormann (as Hitler's private secretary he had enormous influence) and Che Guevara (as Castro's second in command). All were unpopular and criticized by insiders for bypassing the power structure and usurping those within it who merited their position of influence. Meanwhile, outsiders criticized them, holding them responsible for every bad decision made at the top. Peter Mandelson is perhaps the best modern example of a minister-favourite – always so close to the seat of power, yet distrusted within and without; expelled from government in times of difficulty, and brought back quietly once matters had calmed down.

The jealousy of the other courtiers usually ensured the bloody downfall of the favourite. But removing him could sometimes hasten the fall of the king. The three medieval monarchs most known for their favourites – namely Edward II, Richard II and Henry VI – all met the same fate as them in the end. Edward II made Piers Gaveston his 'half-self' and that brought them both down. But on the whole relatively few monarchs were assassinated when there was a minister-favourite to blame instead.

Other examples of lover-favourites included the Earls of Leicester and Essex (both to Elizabeth I) and counsellor-favourites included Cardinal Wolsey and William and Robert Cecil. Some were attractive (the Duke of Buckingham), others unobtrusive bureaucrats (Lord Burghley) and some surprisingly hideous (Robert Cecil). To the outside world these men were haughty demi-gods, yet to their masters they were often servile and seemingly tame. Cardinal Richelieu in particular epitomized this, and was celebrated for his ability to produce tears at will.

One of the most successful courtiers was George Villiers. He became favourite to James I of England, supplanting others and rising swiftly through the peerage (championed in part by enemies of the king's previous favourites) before finally becoming Duke of Buckingham in 1623. But he did not find favour with everyone. He was blamed for a variety of debacles, both marital (concerning the Prince of Wales) and military. Parliament sought to impeach him, but the king protected him. Eventually he was assassinated by one of the soldiers involved in one of the military disasters. Afterwards Thomas Wentworth, Earl of Strafford, remarked, 'it is said at Court there is none now to impute our faults unto.' Ironically, Wentworth himself would be executed for treason by a plainly reluctant Charles I. He had been utterly loyal to the king, but fell foul of Parliament for supporting him in his campaign against the Scots. But this sacrifice only paved the way for the downfall of the king himself.

The execution of Charles I marked the end of the belief in the divine right of kings. Oliver Cromwell was attacking the institution of monarchy as much as anything else, and sought ritually to destroy it by putting the king to death.

Kings had been deposed and killed before, but without the need for a trial. (Edward II and Richard II were both overthrown by Parliament, and killed, but their assassins remained hidden. The usurpers wanted rid of the kings, but not the monarchy, which was preserved.) This ritual had different effects though, in that, as the king died, a martyr was born. The crowd rushed forward looking for trophies, dipping their shirts and handkerchiefs in his blood. A small industry in royal relics developed, which was not what Cromwell had intended.

Towards the end of Charles' rule the country was torn apart by fighting, with few prospects of peace in 1642. The king's enemies saw him as an agent of the Antichrist, and regarded these as the End Days. Reformers sought to ban church decorations and stained-glass windows, all seen as idolatrous. The Book of Revelation, describing what was to come, gained in popularity and fuelled the witch craze. Senior officers in Charles' army had met at a prayer meeting in Windsor Castle in April 1648. They saw the renewed outbreak of war as divine retribution for their sins, and the king as the embodiment of evil. They resolved to destroy him in an open ceremony, expiating the evil that afflicted the country. This was justified with the verse from the Book of Numbers: 'for blood it defileth the land: and the land cannot be cleansed of the blood that is shed therein, but by the blood of him that shed it' (Numbers, 35:33).

The death of Charles was a precursor to that of Louis XIV after the French Revolution. Robespierre had stated that Louis must die so France could live (though the French king was dethroned before he was executed, unlike Charles). This idea of ritual killing stretches back to Romulus killing Remus and founding Rome. The two trials of Charles and Louis paved the way for a series of political ones throughout the twentieth century, as victors dispensed their version of justice to their defeated foes in the court room.

THE CHRISTIAN
SCAPEGOAT

Like all religions, Christianity's primary challenge over the centuries – apart from seeking to defeat its rivals in the spiritual marketplace and establish a monopoly – has been how to explain the existence of evil. The scapegoat is central to that process. Given its God's omnipotence, Christianity has struggled to account for the terrible things that happen in this world. Even now the Church cannot fully agree on why God could allow evil. In the eighteenth century, David Hume famously raised the issue thus, writing of God: 'Is he willing to prevent evil, but not able? Then he is impotent. Is he able, but not willing? Then he is malevolent. Is he both able and willing? Whence then is evil?' And Hume had a point. Whence indeed? What use is our service to the Lord if he is unable or unwilling to intervene on our behalf? God's representatives on earth have lived like kings for centuries, while the people they served suffered. But why? This was a question they needed to answer.

One explanation came in the form of the Devil, as a

counterpart to the Christian God – his scapegoat even. In ancient times there had been just one god, a sky god. But he was felt to be too inaccessible and so was gradually replaced by a troupe of lesser gods, who were capable of both good and bad deeds, as epitomized by the gods of ancient Greece. Even then we expected too much from them. At the beginning of *The Odyssey*, Zeus laments man's tendency to blame the gods rather than himself:

> What a lamentable thing it is that men should blame the gods and regard *us* as the source of their troubles, when it is their own wickedness that brings them sufferings worse than any which Destiny allots them.

In pagan antiquity, gods and mortals were much closer, so it was not unusual for the former to appear to the latter (whereas these days it is generally a sign of 24-carat lunacy). These pagan gods were territorial; they would only have jurisdiction in a particular area, and so it was usual to worship the local deities when you were travelling.[18] There was always room for another god alongside them, just so long as that god was not seeking to displace them. This is why Christianity managed to have considerable overlap with traditional pagan religions in its early years, as it expanded westwards into Europe. Religion being mainly about ritual then (as opposed to faith), Christianity could complement, rather than compete with, the local animist beliefs and practices. Their cults were preserved, and worship of Diana, Hecate and others continued, along with their more lurid rituals. The Church reasoned that it would deal with these at a later date; the priority was to get the Christian message across, and the heathen lasciviousness could be stamped out afterwards.

In the thousand years after the first Christian Roman emperor, Constantine I, Christianity spread widely across Europe. Evangelicals tended to be of noble status and so they approached their fellow nobles, who imposed the new religion on their subjects. Christianity had to repackage itself as it expanded to compete effectively with the local beliefs. The concept of original sin[19] lacked the appeal and simplicity of the pagan horned god and his Nordic counterpart Loki (being too complex an idea, particularly when it came to explaining failed harvests and the like), and so the Devil was brought in as a figure of blame.

Previously the Devil had not been a cornerstone of the faith. In the Old Testament, he barely appears and is a minor figure. In Islam, Satan is also a minor figure, but a foolish one, more like Loki than the Christian Devil. He is a relatively harmless trickster and will be forgiven on the final day. Karen Armstrong points out that the epithet 'the Great Satan' for America is derisory but not as condemnatory as we in the West might think. The Christian God is responsible for both good and evil, as he is in the Jewish faith. As a result God's actions are cruel and willful, from Noah's ark and the flood, to Sodom and Gomorrah and the killing of the first-born in Egypt. Malak Yahweh was his messenger, responsible for God's destruction and bringing pestilence and other curses from him. But the messenger could only insulate God so much from the harshness of the punishments he inflicted on mankind. It became harder and harder to justify his actions and the scale of them made blaming our human weakness almost impossible. And so, in the New Testament, evil was passed onto the Devil. From a literary perspective, God and Jesus need the Devil as a counterpart, just as Sherlock Holmes needs Moriarty, or James Bond Blofeld. The New Testament wouldn't be the same without him. He acted as a signifier for evil and, being responsible for it, let God and ourselves off the hook.

Since then the Devil has flitted in and out of fashion with the Church. In the popular imagination, he blossomed, gaining more and more names – Satan, Lucifer,

Mephistopheles, Beelzebub, Leviathan, the Prince of Darkness ... Once he had been portrayed as an angel, but he swiftly took animal form, as a goat originally (echoing the classical figure of Pan, and the rising Christian fear of sexuality) and later as a serpent, snake or wolf. Soon he became a hybrid, with elements of each creature as well as human characteristics. He might have the legs of a chicken, or be covered in boils and scars. But whatever his appearance, scarcely any of it originated in scripture. Instead his appearance echoed those of pagan figures such as the horned god. John Milton portrayed Satan in *Paradise Lost* as an archangel who turned against God, and changed him from a grotesque figure, who played tricks upon mankind, into a terrible one. For him, it was 'Better to reign in Hell than to serve in Heaven.' This idea of fallen angels is present in the Bible, in the Epistle of Jude and the Second Epistle of Peter. They were held back by the Lord to await final judgement and so roamed among men on Earth, spying out their weaknesses and testing them by, say, putting fossils in the ground, or these days by publishing books by Richard Dawkins. These angels could enter living bodies and become witches or wizards. They could reanimate corpses, become ghosts or, more commonly, take possession of animals to serve the Devil.

Even today Christianity is not entirely sure what attitude to have towards the Devil. Modern thinkers such as Freud and Jung might put evil within us, and the majority have adopted this more sophisticated view of evil. But there are still many – mostly the more evangelical branches of Christianity – who agree with the ancients and hold that evil lies outside, and is the work of another being, namely the Devil. It was Zarathustra (thought to have lived in Iran around the tenth century BC) who first developed this concept of a shadowy all-powerful figure of blame. Each being is faced with an army of enemies. Existence is a constant struggle against them, and they are under Satan's control. He is the arch-enemy of mankind who uses the great powers at his disposal to thwart us. Essentially, Zarathustra created the idea of this single figure of blame who is responsible for every ill that we suffer.

Several major religions adopted Zarathustra's beliefs, though his own followers are very few in number these days – the largest centre is Mumbai, with 60,000 adherents. His outlook suited those who hated uncertainty, and favoured extremes instead. It divided the world into friends and foes, and created an environment in which people who were gentle and kind in private life could, in good conscience, condemn others to the stake, or otherwise persecute them for religious reasons. They did not want to know their enemies, or seek to understand them further. This thinking would shape much of history.

There was a downside to blaming everything on the Devil. Karen Armstrong writes in *A History of God* that 'one of the problems of ethical monotheism is that it isolates evil. Because we cannot accept the idea that there is evil in our God, there is a danger that we will not be able to endure it within ourselves. It can then be pushed away and made monstrous and inhuman.' All too often we define evil by pointing at monsters – Hitler, Stalin, Pol Pot – but really evil tends to come in more subtle guises and we create them ourselves.

The Gnostics also believed in the Devil, and saw the Earth as his creation. For this, the Church persecuted them vigorously throughout the second and third centuries AD (this started a tradition that would continue much later with the persecution of the Cathars and others whose beliefs clashed with the official line, culminating in the Crusades and the Inquisition). After the Second Coming didn't materialize the persecution of Christians intensified, and the Gnostics felt that such a hostile world could only be the work of the Devil. They preached self-destruction and martyrdom as a way of reuniting themselves with

God. Had that prevailed, Christianity would have gone the way of untold numbers of loony cults who voluntarily self-destructed (the movement following Jesus was just one of many rival sects at that time). Gnosticism concentrated on salvation – the present being evil – and was an intensely pessimistic belief system. The tendency to pin all wrongdoing on one person was innate to them. To deal with the threat they posed, the Church leaders denounced them as being heretics and servants of Satan, and they were driven out.

It was in a hostile climate such as this that the Book of Revelation – by some distance the Bible's most extreme text – was written. Millenarian beliefs have always emerged in times of great social upheaval, and Revelation is testament to that. It was written at a time when the Jews were fixated upon ridding themselves of their Roman masters, probably when the Emperor Domitian sought brutally to be worshipped. Satan appears in it as a huge red dragon and there is much more about red heifers and numbers of the beast. This is the only book in the Bible in which the issue of 'natural evil' features. The Devil is held responsible for it – from earthquakes to famine and flood. But the Church has always struggled to explain natural evil and has tended to blame it on the sins of man.

Christian thinkers have furiously debated the subject of evil. Irenaeus did not believe in shifting all blame onto an outside force and he passionately argued for the theory of original sin. His idea was that all humans have carried the burden of Adam and Eve's original sin since Satan entered the garden and used the serpent to tempt them. According to Irenaeus, God offered Jesus as a ransom for the souls held by the Devil, but the Devil killed Jesus, who nonetheless inflicted a mortal wound on him. The Devil continued to harbour anger towards humanity, and the attacks suffered by the Church and Christians were proof of that.

St. Augustine also believed in original sin, but linked it with sex, and this view has persisted in Christianity. As a faith it has always lived in fear of sexuality, despite claiming to be the religion of love, and this is largely down to one man and his writings. St. Augustine grew up in North Africa in the fourth century AD. His early life had been, by his own admission, one of unbridled excess. He had a mistress with whom he had a child before getting engaged to another woman. But some form of breakdown, and the Epistles of Paul, convinced him that chastity was the path he should take. He equated original sin with the sexual act, which transmitted that sin from generation to generation. And so he shaped the Christian attitude to sex and women, with far-reaching consequences. It is perhaps worth remembering that Augustine formulated these extraordinarily bleak, even misogynistic, ideas around the time of the fall of Rome, and that informed his outlook and doctrines. He was trying to explain how Christian Rome could fall to pagan Goths.

Other religious leaders of the time had different views. Tertullian was the author of numerous early works of theology in the second century AD, in which he maintained that the Devil was a creature, not a divine being. He was the shadow of God, filling the world with lies, and was present everywhere. Tertullian listed the following demonic activities: astrology, horse-racing, attending the theatre, wearing make-up, taking baths and frequenting taverns. Another scholar of the time, Origen, disagreed and thought that the Devil wanted to be God and that it was pride that had brought about his fall. Origen also believed that our flesh had been corrupted but the spirit was still pure. He castrated himself[20] in a literal attempt to follow the teachings of Christ, so perhaps we should leave his ideas there and move on to the man he sought to emulate – the ultimate Christian scapegoat.

CHRIST THE SCAPEGOAT

'The blood of martyrs is the seed of the church.'

Tertullian

The scapegoat is in many ways the central figure in Christianity. As a faith, it has always lauded its martyrs, even when the need for martyrdom vanished. Anyone could become a martyr, dying in the same way that Christ did. Martyrs were meant to die bravely, their stoicism having a profound effect on onlookers. In doing so they expiated their sin, washing it away with blood, just as the water of baptism did.

Tyndale's scapegoat is just one of many figures in the Bible who is persecuted by the majority. Abel, Joseph, Moses, John the Baptist, the Servant of Yahweh, all underwent death or brutal suffering at the hands of others in the Old Testament. Another victim, Jonah, was chosen by sailors during a storm as the one to be thrown overboard to save the ship. And Tyndale's scapegoat was the biblical forerunner of the greatest victim of all – Jesus, the son of God, who died upon the cross, taking on the sins of mankind. John recorded the High Priest Caiaphas saying that, 'it is better for one man to die for the people, than for the whole nation to be destroyed' and this is one of the central themes of Christianity.

Jesus was the second Adam, and his rise balanced the fall of the first. The idea was that Adam sinned so completely that only Christ could undo the damage by dying on the cross (this 'symmetry' in the Bible is also seen in how the disobedience of Eve is echoed by the obedience of Mary, and the Tree of Life in the Garden of Eden becomes the True Cross). He was seen as the greatest example of a scapegoat by Sir James Frazer, but he was to be the last one. It is written in the Talmud that, after Jesus' crucifixion, God would accept no more sacrifices like those in Leviticus.[21] By dying on the cross for us, he removed the need for further expiation. And unlike many scapegoats, he accepted his fate voluntarily. He was also an example of the scapegoat who was *stronger* than those whose sin he took on. Before his death, though, there were several occasions where he nearly met the scapegoat's end.

In Luke's gospel, there is a passage in which Christ angered a mob in Nazareth with his preaching:

When they heard this everyone in the synagogue was enraged. They sprang to their feet and hustled him out of the town; and they took him up to the brow of the hill their town was built on, intending to throw him down the cliff, but he slipped through the crowd and walked away.

This was an archetypal scene of the mob versus the scapegoat. Forcing the victim off a cliff (incidentally, there is no such cliff in Nazareth) or stoning him were the two ideal ways of committing collective murder. No one person has sole contact with the victim.

In a reversal of this incident, Jesus encounters a man possessed by unclean spirits. Jesus used exorcism as a method of expelling evil. These spirits were in the service of the Devil and would come out when confronted by Christ. But unlike in other rituals, he was able to destroy them rather than merely shift them from one being to another. In the Gospel of Mark, the scene is described thus:

And no sooner had he left the boat than a man with an unclean spirit came out from the tombs toward him ... All night and all day, among the tombs and in the mountains, he would howl and gash himself with stones … Jesus had been saying to him, 'Come out of the man, unclean spirit.' 'What is your name?' Jesus asked. 'My name is legion,' he answered, 'for there are many of us.' And he begged him earnestly not to send them out of the district. Now there was on the mountainside a great herd of pigs feeding, and the unclean spirits begged him, 'Send us to the pigs, let us go into them.' So he gave them leave. With that, the unclean spirits came out and went into the pigs, and the herd of about two thousand pigs charged down the cliff into the lake, and there they were drowned. And when the people heard about it, they were afraid and begged Jesus to leave the neighbourhood.

What is unusual about this scene (apart from the concept of the Son of God) is that, for a moment, the roles were reversed and the multitude fled from the scapegoat, charging over the cliff that usually they would have driven him over. Also, the demoniac stones himself, imitating the fate that the crowd would have inflicted on him. Again Jesus escaped the mob, but he would not do so forever.

Jesus was a political threat to the Romans at a time of great instability. The Romans sought his downfall and had him crucified like a common criminal. But most Christians did not want the Roman Empire as their enemy, and the Passion narratives transfer blame onto the Jewish authorities. The local representative of Roman power, Pontius Pilate, is portrayed as having to condemn Jesus against his own judgement, at the volition of the Jewish Sanhedrin.

After Christ's death his followers believed that evil would be destroyed sooner rather than later. His apostles continued his teaching but, after they died, a whole host of different interpretations sprang up, since Jesus had left behind no writings. But he seemed to suggest that the end of time was coming soon and, as a result, many of his followers were expecting a Second Coming. The Jews rose against the Romans in this belief, fighting a holy war against them between AD 66 and 70. The Messiah failed to come to their aid and they were defeated. In the subsequent search for explanation they turned on each other. Pharisees blamed Sadducees and vice versa, and the Devil was also held responsible.

The centuries after the death of Christ saw extensive persecution of Christians by the Romans.[22] The latter became increasingly fearful as their empire grew weaker and more threatened. At that time Christians were regarded as a minor Jewish sect and lived in expectation of an imminent Apocalypse, so were perhaps less mindful of fitting in with the customs of others. But their togetherness was perceived as sinister, and their rituals shocking, particularly the Eucharist. They were accused of child murder, incest, cannibalism; of worshipping a 'donkey god' and their priests' genitals. All of these accusations would in turn be used by the Church against their enemies, in particular the Jews. Ultimately our imagination is relatively limited when it comes to wickedness, and the authorities trot out the same list of accusations towards minorities they wish to demonize.

The scapegoat figure of Christ is echoed in other religions and is a different, stronger scapegoat than the archetype. This sort takes on the sin of others because it is able to. The Aztecs had Tlazolteotl, the goddess of childbirth, who ate the sins of men once in each individual's life time – much as, in the animal kingdom, mothers might eat the excretions of their young to keep the nest clean. The Hindus have Shiva, who is the only being able to absorb the poison that emerged when the gods churned the Milky Ocean. And there is a Chinese smiling Buddha whose fat stomach can be rubbed as a way of passing human suffering into him. Throughout this, his expression does not change from one of joy. These are all positive figures, full of power, able to take on this burden of sin because they are stronger than others. These religious scapegoats are far removed from the scapegoat as a mere victim.

THE JEWISH SCAPEGOAT

Over the centuries, the Catholic Church has done more than its fair share of demonizing. As so often happens, Christianity suffered persecution when weak, and became the persecutor when strong. The Church was not slow to denigrate its enemies. As it grew in power, its leaders managed to perpetuate the illusion that they were still under threat from dark, malign forces, when really these were just the great threats of war, famine and disease that everyone faced over a thousand years ago. The fear of the Devil was deliberately aroused in Europe, mainly in the eleventh, fourteenth and sixteenth centuries, and this would lead to the extensive persecution of witches. But the power of competing religions, predominantly of the Muslims and Jews, also had to be dealt with. A series of Crusades was launched against the former, though its first victims were in fact the Jews.

To the great indignation of the Christian world, Caliph al-Hâkim of Egypt had brought about the demolition of Constantine's Basilica of the Holy Sepulchre in Jerusalem.

After that, the idea of retaking the Holy Land was born. Gregory VII was the first pope to attempt to launch a Crusade, but he was unsuccessful. Urban II fared better, promising his troops that death on a Crusade would, with repentance and confession, lead to a place in heaven (this encouraging idea would pave the way for the system of indulgences, whose corruption became a major cause of the Reformation).

The Crusaders set out in 1096 but the mission did not begin as Urban had planned. For some of these Crusaders it seemed slightly illogical to travel so far to fight an unknown enemy when the more immediate enemies – the killers of Christ, in fact – were in their midst. They slaughtered the Jewish communities in the Rhine valley, many of whom had lent the money the Crusaders needed to set out on this religious quest in the first place. The Jews aroused resentment for their success and education, and, ultimately, in the hearts of the Christian masses, they still carried the blame for the persecution of Christ. In 1215, at the Fourth Lateran Council, Pope Innocent III had ruled that Jews should wear a yellow patch and a horned cap, marking them out as Christ's murderers. Between the thirteenth and sixteenth centuries they were expelled from France, Italy, England, Bohemia and the Germanic states.

It was only after the French Revolution that they were recognized as citizens of France.[23]

In fifteenth-century Spain the Jews were persecuted by the Inquisition, which expelled those who did not convert to Catholicism. This conversion did not stop them from being considered tainted. They were known as *conversos*, but also, pejoratively, *marranos* – or pigs. It was around this time that the concept of blood as a carrier of racial qualities emerged. Blood became central to anti-Semitic myth. Jewish men were thought to have tails and to menstruate, so they bled and then had to replace the blood, which they did by killing and eating Christian children. The blood-libel accusation would resurface again and again.

The Jews were blamed for a multitude of other ills – principally the Black Death – forcing Pope Clement VI to issue a bull saying the Jews were not responsible. But he could not blame God instead, nor could he blame man for his sins – that would have provided ammunition for those responsible for many of the anti-Semitic attacks, who even accused Jews of poisoning wells and food supplies. Instead, the pope attributed the plague to a misalignment of the planets, which is as close as the Church will ever get to saying that it, like the rest of us, just doesn't know. This was a rare occasion when the Church did not designate a minority as evil-doers.

The conventional resort was to blame heretics, lepers, homosexuals[24] or larger groups such as the Jews, even the female half of the population ...

THE SEXUAL SCAPEGOAT

'But now the woman opened up the cask,
And scattered pains and evils among men.'

Hesiod

The witch hunts of the Middle Ages and afterwards are one of the most spectacular and disturbing examples of blame being misdirected onto the vulnerable. They were driven by a need to find those responsible for small local tragedies (the death or illness of a child or livestock, or any domestic accident), at a time when it was feared that the Devil lurked behind every mishap. The religious instability of the time provided a fertile environment for this persecution, as communities purged themselves of their least respected and economically valuable members, with the full encouragement of the authorities. A mass wave of scapegoating swept through Europe as tens of thousands of women (and some men) were accused of witchcraft and burned, hanged or drowned. A fear of witchcraft was nothing new however, and the real causes for this misogyny lay much deeper, in the very earliest mythologies, enshrined in the stories of creation.

The ancients believed that we originally existed in a state of purity, and for some, this meant a world without women. According to Greek mythology, men had lived side by side with the gods, free from pain and labour and disease. Woman was an afterthought, as she was in the Bible. Pandora was only sent by Zeus as a punishment to men, after Prometheus had stolen fire from the gods, and as an accompaniment to his entrails being pecked at daily by vultures before regrowing overnight. Pandora brought with her a large jar which she was told never to open, but she did, and so released all the evils in the world. Since then mankind has been condemned to work, grow old, weaken and finally die. This story was first written down by Hesiod in the eighth century BC and its message is echoed elsewhere in Greek mythology – from the Furies and the Gorgons to Scylla and Charybdis (who were both originally sea nymphs), Circe, Medusa and Medea. All reinforce this original expression of feminine evil.

The goddess Atë was responsible for infatuation as well as mischief, delusion and blind folly. She was the daughter of Zeus and Eris, the goddess of strife. Atë was thought to have triggered the Trojan War by turning up uninvited to the wedding of Peleus and Thetis (though some versions have it that Eris provoked the Judgement of Paris). There, she encouraged Hera, Aphrodite and Athena to fight over a golden apple inscribed 'For the Fairest'.[25] The argument went on and on, and in the end Zeus sent them to a shepherd, Paris, for his verdict. Hera offered him Europe and Asia to rule, while Athena promised him the gifts of wisdom and war, and Aphrodite the prize of the most beautiful woman in the world – Helen, wife of Menelaus. Paris duly chose Aphrodite as the fairest, and gave her the apple. And so Helen fell in love with him, and they fled to Troy together, with all the tragedy that came after.

Atë was also later thought to have caused Achilles' argument with Agamemnon, who blamed her for his infatuation with the girl he had taken from Achilles. Euripides wrote:

Delusion, the eldest daughter of Zeus: the accursed
Who deludes all and leads them astray …
… took my wife away from me.
She has entangled others before me.

However, in his final plays Euripides allowed that evil and stupidity could not be attributed solely to external causes, to goddesses such as Atë or the intervention of another being. Instead, evil resides at our core and that must be confronted.

After Pandora came Helen of Troy as the focal point of Ancient Greek misogyny. Famously she was blamed for the bloodshed of the Trojan War; it was her beauty that provoked it, not Menelaus or the Greek leaders who supported him. Ultimately, her husband had to get her back partly because his kingship depended on it. Another version had it that Zeus used Helen to cause a war to thin out a population that was threatening to become unmanageable. Euripides wrote in his play about Helen that Zeus 'might lighten mother earth of her myriad hosts of men.'

As their mythology testifies, this fear of women was endemic to Greek society. In Athens in the sixth century BC, women had the legal status of children, just as, in early Jewish law, women were not regarded as fit witnesses for legal matters. It is ironic that, according to the three Gospel accounts, the resurrection of Jesus was only witnessed by women. Greek women were mostly confined to their own part of the house and were given no formal education. No Athenian citizen was allowed to enslave another but there was an exception that a father could sell his unmarried daughter into slavery should she lose her virginity before marriage. A child was thought to have reached its full potential by being born male, whereas baby girls were 'mutilated' versions of the male, according to Aristotle. He believed that women were inferior to men – they did not go bald, so were more childlike, and also had fewer teeth. The twentieth-century British philosopher Bertrand Russell commented of this, 'Aristotle would never have made this mistake if he had allowed his wife to open her mouth once in a while.' Meanwhile, the Greek playwright Menander wrote in the third or fourth century BC: 'He who teaches letters to his wife is ill advised: he's giving additional poison to a snake.'

The snake is also, of course, central to the Christian creation myth of Adam and Eve in the Garden of Eden. There, too, woman's disobedience caused us to fall from grace. Eve, like Pandora, disobeyed: 'The serpent did beguile me and I did eat.' In doing so, she awoke man to the misery and hardness of life, and for that she has not been forgiven. Over the centuries, male leaders have used the myth that woman's disobedience is to blame for the world's ills to justify their patriarchal power. Mesopotamian and Celtic myths did not contain an equivalent of the Fall of Man – an Eve or Pandora figure –

but it was the Greek and Christian traditions that most shaped Western attitudes towards women. These asked man to believe that he sprung up fully formed and independent of woman. And Christianity led the way. While Jesus' attitude towards women was new and enlightened, showing far more compassion and respect to them than was usual at the time, the Old Testament is full of blame and misogyny. In Ecclesiastes it is written: 'From a garment cometh a moth, and from woman wickedness.'[26]

This should not be that surprising. Christianity is, after all, a religion with an unusually severe attitude towards sex. The Church was run by men, and so it blamed women. It does not accept its central female figure as a sexual one, casting her as a virgin. It demands celibacy from its priests however that may pervert the sexuality of some of them. And it is only beginning to allow the role of contraception as a way of preventing the spread of AIDS in Africa. Adherence to these strictures dates back to the writings of St. Augustine and other early Christian leaders – the ideas of the fourth century AD still sold to a populace in the early twenty-first century.

Eve was vilified by these leaders, but not in the Bible. They made her responsible for the fall of man, for his expulsion from Eden.[27] Tertullian wrote of woman:

You are the devil's gateway; you are the unsealer of that forbidden tree; you are the first deserter of Divine Law. You are she who persuaded him whom the devil was not valiant enough to attack. You destroyed so easily God's image, man.

Tertullian did not blame the Jews or the Romans for the death of Christ; instead, he blamed the female sex. This all led towards the theory of original sin, which held that the Virgin Mary was the only human other than Jesus to be free from it. The only way in which women could hope to follow, even to emulate, her was through chastity.

Not even chastity could save a woman who stood out. Hypatia was born in Alexandria between AD 350 and 370, and is one of the most exceptional women in history. She was proficient in (and taught) philosophy, geometry and astronomy, surpassing the philosophers of her time. She was also admired for her character. Allegedly, when one of her smitten students exposed himself to her, she presented him with her bloodstained underwear as a way of dousing his passion. The local Christians resented her, despite her obvious gifts and virtue, and soon saw an opportunity to bring her down through blame.

Bishop Cyril of Alexandria had roused a mob against

the local Jews, urging them to sack their homes and turn their synagogues into churches. When the Imperial Prefect objected, the crowd not only attacked him, but accused Hypatia of having bewitched him into supporting the Jews. Her intellectual and musical accomplishments were seen as clear signs that she was a witch, and so one of Bishop Cyril's followers led a mob to her academy. They dragged her to a church, stripped her and, according to some accounts, skinned her with broken tiles and oyster shells. Then they burned her remains. Her murderers were never prosecuted, and Cyril, who had set all of this in motion by denouncing her in a sermon, rose higher and higher in the Church, eventually being canonized. It remains one of the most shameful episodes in Christian history. But the attitudes behind it are not unique. One of the reasons for the persecution of the Cathars[28] was their 'heresy' of allowing women to play a more prominent part in society. Denied worldly influence, the only great powers that women were credited with at this time were supernatural ones.

From the fifth century to the fifteenth, witchcraft was widely thought to exist.[29] It might be difficult for the modern mind to comprehend, but this belief was deeply ingrained and widespread. Nothing was ever seen to have happened by chance and almost everything bad that took place was the result of witchcraft. Just occasionally misfortune was God's punishment for our sins, but more often than not it was the work of some neighbouring hag. They were the intermediaries between laymen and the Devil, the evil counterpart to the priest. They had plenty of assistance in their foul deeds. It was thought that the earth was overrun by demons, and their number was added to by the souls of wicked men and women, and of stillborn children. Male demons were incubi, female ones succubi. They could make themselves lovely or hideous. According to the fifteenth-century Dutch scholar Johann Weyer, there were 7,405,926 of them, divided into 72 battalions, each led by a prince or a captain. It was possible to breathe these demons in, and so they could get lodged in your body and thus cause illness and pain.

Witchcraft was a collective endeavour; instead of individual witches running around casting spells, oblivious to each other, there was a shared ethos, with rituals and nightly meetings, or Sabbaths. It was this idea of an overall plot that gave the witch hunt such power and impetus. The witch hunters were looking for the enemy within, rather than finding an external hate figure, though he existed in the form of the Devil. He was not allowed to influence man directly and so used these intermediaries to test the souls of men. Rid the world of witches, the thinking went, and you reduced the spread of evil.

For the anti-witch inquisitors, feminine carnality was at the heart of witchcraft, spreading and compounding our original sin. At their Sabbaths, the witches would regularly meet and have sex with the Devil. There was always a great deal of curiosity about this – was sex with him more enjoyable than sex with a man? The confessions of suspected witches (often under torture) became ever more lurid in their descriptions of the unholy member, which was like that of a mule or a man's arm and uncomfortably cold (most of what was known of the Devil was information extracted, and shaped, by torture). The Sabbaths would take place at a crossroads or by a lake, leaving the ground all scorched afterwards. In France and England, witches rode broomsticks to get there; in Italy and Spain the Devil carried them, having assumed the form of a goat, which was his favourite shape. And it was as a goat that he would host the Sabbath. The witches and wizards would dance until they collapsed, then any newcomers would kiss the goat's hindquarters, deny their salvation and spit on the Bible. They would recount their sins, and if they hadn't committed enough would be reprimanded by the Devil who would flog them with thorns or a scorpion. Then proceedings might be rounded off with a dance of toads while the Devil played the bagpipes.

Witches were believed to target fertility above all else, whether it be in humans or crops. For so much of history, procreation has been a relative mystery, and a favoured explanation for its failure was the ugly old woman coming between the beautiful young lovers. She could do so in surprising ways. According to the *Malleus Maleficarum* (of which more later) witches often stole penises, 'in great numbers, as many as 20 or 30 together, and put them in a bird's nest or shut them up in a box, where they move themselves, like living members, and eat oats and corn.' As proof of this, the authors offered the following story: 'A certain man tells that, when he lost his member, he approached a certain witch to ask her to restore his health. She told the afflicted man to climb a certain tree, and that he might take whichever member he liked out of a nest in which there were several members. And when he tried to take a big one, the witch said, "You must not take that one," adding, "because it belonged to a parish priest".' Here, an old anti-clerical joke was adopted as anti-witch propaganda.[30]

Up until the early fourteenth century, accusations of witchcraft tended to be made by members of the political classes against each other as they jostled for power. In 1317, Pope John XXII had a French bishop burned at the stake, accused of using witchcraft in a plot against him. King Edward II also claimed that his political enemies used witchcraft against him. The common people were rarely affected by such concerns. But witchcraft was a charge that was so easily brought and so hard to refute that the powerful could use it against their enemies whenever they wanted to crush them and had no firm crime to pin on them. It was used as a pretext for the violent persecution of individuals and communities whose real transgressions were entirely political or religious.

A prominent example of this was the extermination of the Stedinger in 1234. They had lived peacefully with a remarkable degree of civil and religious freedom, but found themselves harassed by the Archbishop of Bremen, among others. They refused to pay the taxes and tithes demanded of them and rose up to drive out their oppressors. Eventually the archbishop appealed to Pope Gregory IX for help. But the first invasion was repelled. The pope called for a crusade to put down this den of iniquity, accusing the Stedinger of witchcraft, devil worship and the usual litany of crimes. A great army was raised on the back of this, and the rebels were defeated. A similar process was used against the Templars (who were accused of child murder, sodomy, etc.) between 1307 and 1313. They too were exterminated (there was also a financial imperative here; the French kings seized the Templar wealth). The thirteenth century had seen great outbreaks of religious fervour – including the Flagellants who marched from town to town in their bloodstained processions – and these extreme sects could turn against the Church as much as they could be absorbed by it. So there was a need, more than ever, for the Church to find a common enemy.

The arrival of the Black Death and its spread across Europe made this all the more urgent. At least 30 per cent of the population in Europe would die of this plague, which killed an estimated 25 million victims. Jews were the first to be blamed for its arrival, and many of their communities were exterminated by vengeful mobs. Muslims and lepers were also held responsible. The witch craze was beginning to take root, and witches would be added to the Catholic Church's roster of useful scapegoats as they exhausted the others, quite literally, by exterminating them. Previously there had been incidents of witchcraft and subsequent trials, but no systematic campaign to deal with witches. It took the Church's involvement to achieve this. The fourteenth century was – like the fifth century BC in Greece and the third century AD in Rome – a time of calamity, of plagues and wars, when fear and uncertainty were rife. New forms of belief challenged the once omnipotent Church and its monopoly on truth. It was no time to be out of the ordinary, particularly as a woman. For the next couple of centuries the witch craze ran freely. There would be so many trials for witchcraft that other crimes were overlooked. And the more witches the authorities burned, the more they found to burn.

At the fore in the witch hunt were two Dominican Inquisitors, Heinrich Kramer and Jacob Sprenger. They had convinced Pope Innocent VIII of the very real threat posed to the Church and to civilization by witchcraft, and so obtained almost unlimited powers from him. In 1484 Kramer had been investigating a case in Ravensburg, in Germany. Eight women were due to face trial, accused of 'causing injury to people and animals, and for raising "tempests" to destroy the harvest.' Subsequently over 20 witches were burned at the stake. Afterwards he moved east with his witch-hunters but met with different treatment in Innsbruck. There the bishop considered Kramer senile and dangerous, and set the accused witches free. So Kramer and Sprenger sought more power from the pope.

Later that year Innocent VIII issued a papal bull declaring open season on witches:

> And at the instigation of the Enemy of Mankind they do not shrink from committing and perpetrating foulest abominations and filthiest excuses to the deadly peril of their own souls ... Wherefore we ... decree and enjoin that the aforesaid inquisitors [Kramer and Sprenger] be empowered to proceed to the just correction, imprisonment, and punishment of any persons, without let or hindrance, in every way ...

Sprenger was alleged to have burned over five hundred witches in a single year, yet was also the founder of the Confraternity of the Holy Rosary, set up to honour the Virgin Mary. He and Kramer were most famous for the book they wrote together, the *Malleus Maleficarum* (known also as the 'Hammer of the Witches'). This became one of the most read books of the time and is probably the most misogynistic text ever published. It first came out in 1486 and, like the Bible, it benefited from the new technology of the printing press for its success; there were 13 different Latin editions in print by 1523, 15 German editions printed up to 1700 and 11 French. Its principal message was that witches, having struck a pact with the Devil, were responsible for all misfortunes, and it offered much advice on how to deal with them.

The authors drew heavily on the Bible and invoked its authority. Most famously, they quoted the line from Exodus where it was written, 'Thou shalt not suffer a witch to live'. The misogyny of the *Malleus Maleficarum* was overt – women are the 'more credulous' sex, being feeble, carnal, insatiable. A woman is 'a liar by nature' and 'an imperfect animal', 'a foe to friendship, an inescapable punishment, an evil of nature painted in fair colours.' And so on. Kramer and Sprenger helped move witchcraft from being an ecclesiastical sin to being an actual crime in the eyes of the law, on the grounds of the damage done by witches to the property of others. The book stated that witches will not admit to being witches and must therefore be tortured. 'Mind that [they] generally deny the question'. Witches 'will not be able to weep'; a truly absurd claim, since the trials were punctuated by frequent outbursts of weeping from the terrified and brutalized suspects (courtrooms at that time were chaotic places, where the testimony and statements were often drowned out by noise). During proceedings, the feet and foreheads of the accused would be examined with particular care for signs of cloven hooves or horns, since witches and sorcerers were thought to have very close links to the goat. The rest of their bodies would also be scrutinized for any mark that might denote involvement with witchcraft. Here even the slightest physical abnormality could be seized on as firm evidence of Satanic allegiance.

Legal representation was almost impossible in these cases. A previous pope, Paul II, had permitted the use of torture to extract confessions when witchcraft was suspected. The prevailing view was that it was a crime so terrible that normal standards of evidence need not apply. Witchcraft was a *crimen exceptum*, and proof was so hard to find that regular legal procedure could not be followed. There were numerous methods of torture, notably the witches' chair and bridle. A suspect's feet and legs could be crushed, or their genitals burned. Sleep deprivation would also be used. The Church itself would not carry out the sentence of death. Instead, as in the animal trials that feature in the next chapter, they would pass the culprits over to the civil authorities, usually with a meaningless plea for mercy to be shown. The execution would be carried out, for that is how most witch trials ended.

A witch was, in 80 per cent of cases, a woman. Was this purely the result of a patriarchal, misogynistic society? In many ways it was – men were thought to be stronger, both physically and morally, and in matters of 'reason'. Women were deemed more vulnerable to the Devil's wiles. Like Eve, they were 'first in sin'. And the women accused were usually not part of a male-led household, so they had no male figure to protect them. Women accused women too, and could comprise between 30 to 40 per cent of witnesses. Almost all communities at that time would have had a pool of possible witches. They would be older women who had, by the time they were in their forties or fifties, built up a reputation for witchcraft. Many of them were on bad terms with their children and spouses, or they might have been widowed, and so were a financial burden on the community.

An accusation of witchcraft would most likely come from someone you knew rather than a stranger. There were three principal types of accusers – middle-aged women, men in their twenties and early thirties, and teenage girls; usually individuals who were going through a particularly turbulent phase of their life. A community with around a hundred households was the typical backdrop for a witch drama. These cases were almost always firmly rooted in local personal relations. First there would be a quarrel of some kind. Then, one terrible event – whether it be the death or illness of a child, adult, or of livestock – would gradually turn popular opinion against someone, as the mood darkened and turned to blame. Once an individual voiced this feeling that someone was responsible, then the accusation could be formalized, witnesses found, and a case brought against the suspect. When the trial was over (and the suspect found guilty), there would be a great sense of togetherness, now the difficult person had been eliminated. Order was felt to have been restored.

These isolated incidents were one thing. A witch hunt was something totally different, however, and outbreaks of this mania took place all over Europe. For it to occur there needed to be a popular, legal and political belief in witchcraft. Where torture was banned, witch-hunting was rarer. These hunts mostly happened in what was then the Holy Roman Empire, whose structure lent itself to moral panic; with no strong overall leadership and small fragmented states, witch-hunting sprang up in the gaps. Many major witch hunts happened along religious fault lines, where there had previously been conflicts between faiths or sects.

The papacy was at its most excitable when leading the fight against witchcraft. Innocent VIII became pope in 1485 and did as much as anyone to fuel it. His bull of 1488 called upon Europe to rescue Christianity from this 'sea of witches.' In every country, he appointed inquisitors with the power to convict and punish. Pope John XXII was also obsessed with witchcraft and had added it to the list of heresies in 1320. He appointed bishops who shared his fears and one of them, the Bishop of Ossory in Ireland, led the first trial of a woman accused of having sex with the Devil. Lady Alice Kyteler was a very wealthy inhabitant of Kilkenny, where she lived with her fourth husband. He had recently fallen ill. She was accused of poisoning him and of having disposed of her previous three husbands through witchcraft. This accusation came from her children who felt that she favoured her son from her first marriage. She was charged with these deaths, of obtaining her fortune through sorcery, and also of running an anti-Christian sect which made potions to harm Catholics using the swaddling clothes and brains of dead babies. Many of those who testified against her were her debtors. Lady Kyteler managed to escape to England the night before she was due to be executed but her maid Petronilla didn't. The inquisitors tortured her, and she duly confessed to having witnessed her mistress having intercourse with the Devil (who had assumed the form of three black men) and to having acted as a go-between. Petronilla was one of only two people burned in Ireland as a witch.

In the decades before the Reformation, the Catholic clergy used the charge of witchcraft against Protestants. If an accusation of heresy didn't stick, then one of witchcraft often would. In time the Lutherans and Calvinists came to believe as firmly in witches as the Catholics had (once again, the persecuted became the persecutors). Luther and Calvin might have quarreled with Rome over everything else, but not witchcraft, in which they shared a firm belief. The force of the witch hunts came partly from the intensity of the clashes between Protestants and Catholics as the Reformation and Counter-Reformation raged.

The major witch hunts took place in Germany, Switzerland, north-east France and southern Holland, with lesser epidemics striking England, Scotland, Spain, central and southern France, northern Italy and Scandinavia. The witch mania peaked between 1580 and 1650, the 20 years from 1610 being perhaps the worst. Economic depression, as the peasants suffered from a move to a more communal system of agriculture, added to the political and religious turmoil and created a volatile atmosphere.

The Church's inquisitors were keen to ascertain the size of the task ahead of them, and the strength of the enemy they faced. From their questioning of suspects they tried to work out how many witches there were to pursue, just as historians today struggle to agree on how many witches were burned. In 1570, it was calculated that there were 300,000 witches in France, at a time when the entire population of that country was around 15 million. In other words, two per cent of the population was believed to be attending the witches' Sabbaths and kissing the goat's hindquarters. Around that time Henri Boguet, a judge and demonologist, calculated that there were 1.8 million witches in Europe.

The figures of witches executed have been equally exaggerated. At one point it was claimed that over nine million people were killed. Now it seems more likely that this figure is between 40,000 and 50,000.[31] The most reliable figures suggest that a thousand witches were killed in Britain, half of them in Scotland; 5,000 in Switzerland;[32] 4,000 in France; and 20,000 in Germany. More than these numbers were put on trial – the average conviction rate was 50 per cent, though at the height of the witch craze in

Germany an accusation was tantamount to death. Elsewhere the judges were a little more sceptical of the cases being brought before them, but not by much.

In sixteenth-century France, fires for burning witches blazed brightly in every town. In a typical trial of the time, the husband of an accused witch could testify that his wife had been in bed with him at the time of the alleged witches' Sabbath, but it would be in vain, and she would find herself on the pyre. In 1573 Gilles Garnier was convicted of being a witch *and* a werewolf. He was a loner who lived in the woods with his wife and was accused of having killed several small children – there having been several local instances of children being attacked by wolves. In one case the wolf was thought to have looked like Garnier. He was burned at the stake, having had to pay for the costs of the prosecution. In another case in Auvergne in 1588, a hunter was attacked by a wolf in the woods. He fought it off, severing its paw as he did so. Back at his host's house, he produced the paw, which had turned into a woman's hand, with rings on its fingers. His host duly identified it as that of his wife and she was burned at the stake. In Constance, Switzerland, in 1487, two wretched old women were put to the rack, having been accused of causing a severe storm. Under torture, they confessed to that and much besides. They admitted to having met the Devil often, and having sold their souls to him. The register at Constance reads '*convicta et combusta*'.

There was a rare case of witches being acquitted in Paris in 1589. Fourteen women were accused and closely examined, while naked, by four commissioners who were also doctors. They pricked the suspects all over, to test for insensitivity to pain, which was a key sign of witchcraft. But they found them to be 'very poor, stupid people, and some of them insane. Many of them were quite indifferent about life, and one or two desired death as a relief from their sufferings.'[33] They were seen as being more in need of treatment than punishment and so, in an unusual act of leniency, were sent home. Today these 'witches' would be treated by psychiatrists. The reality is that the accused were often unfortunate, slightly deluded women who fell foul of their neighbours in some way, and were denounced as witches – a charge from which there was no coming back.

These witch-hunts were the perfect opportunity for the downtrodden members of society to be noticed and to make their mark. Those accused of possessing abnormal powers were sometimes members of the élite, but usually they were uneducated and unintelligent people whose imagination had conquered their reason.[34] Sometimes they did start believing the accusations made against them, of possessing dark powers, which they then tried to use against their enemies. This added a terrible irony to the tragedy and assisted their accusers greatly.

The main witch-hunters were the Church and its clerics, led by the pope and his bishops. But others assisted them – leaders and bureaucrats and self-styled witch finders. Bodinus was a leading example of the latter in seventeenth-century Germany. He believed that, 'He who is accused of sorcery should never be acquitted, unless the malice of the prosecutor be clearer than the sun; for it is so difficult to bring full proof of this secret crime, that out of a million of witches not one would be convicted if the usual course were followed.' Henri Boguet styled himself 'The Grand Judge of Witches for the Territory of St Claude' and drew up a code of practice for witch trials. Evidence that would be inadmissible for normal crimes could be used, including from children or from people of notoriously bad or unreliable character.

To begin with, the continental witch craze did not take hold in England with quite the same ferocity as it had in mainland Europe. Witchcraft was first made a crime in England by Henry VIII in 1541, but not until the accession of Elizabeth I was it acknowledged as a serious offence.

Clerics came back from their continental exile alarmed by the perceived threat of witchcraft (in England, there was always a link between witch-hunting and fear of Catholicism).

The Scots embraced witch-hunting with great enthusiasm, combining the burning of suspects with public banquets of celebration. King James VI was a noted obsessive. He was convinced that witches were trying to assassinate him, and even wrote a book on the subject entitled *Daemonologie*. He led the North Berwick witch hunt in 1590 after he had nearly drowned while sailing back from Denmark with his bride. In a story that reads more like a poem by Edward Lear than a conspiracy to murder a king, Cellie Duncan was accused of witchcraft and of having whipped up the storm that nearly drowned James. Under torture, she implicated nearly 40 others, who were also interrogated. They all confessed to having met the Devil in North Berwick and to conspiring with him against his greatest enemy, the king. After their meeting they set to sea in a sieve with a cat that the Devil had given them. They threw this creature in the water and so caused the storm. They confessed to ever more unlikely crimes, testing even the king's willingness to believe, yet were found guilty and executed. After that, the witch craze properly took hold in Scotland, with an acquittal rate of under one per cent. Many of those accused of witchcraft confessed, preferring death to a possible acquittal and the endless persecution for being a witch. One such victim said, 'I made up my confession ... choosing rather to die than to live.'

When James acceded to the throne of England his people were well aware of his glorious deeds. An act against witches was passed in his first Parliament in 1604 stating that they should be burned 'alive and quick'. Under Charles I the witch persecution declined but during the Civil War there was a revival. This was a time when the population was worried about impending disaster. The Apocalypse was expected by many, and a solar eclipse in August 1645 was seen as a sign of this End Time. The general feeling was that Satan knew he didn't have much time available and so had unleashed all his evil minions. More and more sects sprang up and there were countless strange reports – of a woman giving birth to a headless baby, of the corpse of a 'profane-speaking man' being dug up and fed to dogs, and of a pond turning to blood.

It was in this climate of fear that Matthew Hopkins emerged. He was the self-styled Witchfinder General, responsible for a large proportion of England's witch deaths. He had grown up in rural Suffolk, the son of a local minister. He was a Puritan, and is described often as a gentleman (an odd appellation for a man who killed women for a living). Little is known about his early life. He may have practised as a solicitor at one point, but the evidence for this is slight. He was said to have made witch-hunting his calling after overhearing witches discussing their meetings with the Devil, and claimed that they then sent one of their imps to destroy him. He moved from town to town in Essex and East Anglia, exploiting the general chaos and lack of overall rule. He would let it be known that he was approaching an area, where parishes would usually welcome him, the local authorities or landowners fearful of attracting a charge of witchcraft themselves. Once there he would set up with his assistant, John Stearne, another devout Puritan, and conduct surveys and question suspects.

Hopkins' first victim was Elizabeth Clarke of Manningtree, an old woman who had fallen foul of her neighbours. The wife of a local tailor had fallen ill and he had gone to consult a fortune-teller, who had accused Clarke. Suspicions of witchcraft had long surrounded her, and Hopkins was commissioned by the local magistrates to question her, on the suspicion of witchcraft. Torture was illegal in England at that time, but Hopkins used sleep deprivation and 'walking' (exhausting the suspect by marching them round their cell). A suspect might be asked to recite the Lord's Prayer; one tiny stumble or slip (and just imagine how nervous they would have been) was taken as a sure sign of guilt. A detailed examination of the suspect's body would be made, for something that might be the Devil's Mark. A third nipple was particularly sought after as a sign that the witch had suckled the Devil and his imps. These imps would visit in animal form, so the suspect would be tied up and placed on a stool as watchers waited for them to come. A fly landing on her would be evidence of guilt. The suspect would also be 'pricked' with pins and knives, as the interrogators looked for parts of the body that felt no pain. This would be seen as a definite sign of witchery.

After three days of being watched Elizabeth Clarke confessed to having had 'carnall copulation' with the Devil and a lot else besides. She was made to implicate many other witches and this led to England's largest witch trial (assuming there aren't going to be any more), in Chelmsford. Twenty-nine suspects, all women, were in the dock, along with a few others accused of more conventional crimes. Hopkins took the stand as the first

113

witness against the first batch to be charged. He told of imps disguised as ferrets and rabbits and toads, and described how one attacked his own greyhound. The suspects' confessions were read out and all five were found guilty and sentenced to death by hanging.[35] Not everyone was convinced of the guilt of these witches.[36] Arthur Wilson, the steward for the Earl of Warwick, saw only poor, unhappy old women, who were suffering from various delusions. One of them was 84 and died a month after the trial, probably from the plague, defeating the hangman.

Hopkins did not only target women. One of his victims was an 80-year-old vicar, John Lowes, who had been in dispute with his parishioners for some time. He was a Catholic, when they would have preferred a Puritan, and was by all accounts an argumentative man, believed to have struck one of his parishioners in a row. When he defended a member of his congregation as being no more of a witch than he was, this was taken as an admission of guilt. He was arrested on a charge of witchcraft and questioned by Hopkins. As with a female suspect, he was stripped and examined for the Devil's mark. He was deprived of sleep and walked forcibly around his cell until he collapsed from exhaustion. After days of this, and in a state of hallucination, he confessed to a variety of crimes, including sending an imp to sink a ship that had gone down in a recent storm. He was hanged alongside a number of other convicted witches, and this execution was widely attended. Lowe was supposed to have boasted of a charm that would stop him from being hanged, so many turned up to see the truth of this.

Hanging was the preferred method of execution. Almost no witches were burned in England, despite the popular belief that they were. Trial by fire was three times as expensive and so used sparingly, mostly for heretics rather than witches.[37] It also required more raw materials. When Mary Lakeland was burned at the stake for murdering her husband she was lowered into a barrel of pitch, chained to a post and surrounded by straw and brushwood. It was much cheaper to build gallows and hang several witches together.

The economics of witch-hunting are fascinating and highly relevant. When Hopkins went to Aldeburgh, the whole process including the trial cost £40. This was a seventh of the town's budget for the entire year. The carpenter was paid £1 to erect the gallows and the executioner received 11 shillings. Meanwhile, Hopkins was paid 20 shillings per conviction – so there was a good financial reason to find suspects guilty. His record was having 19 witches hung in a day. Hopkins complained about his expenses, believing that he should receive more for his efforts, but 20 shillings was a month's wages for a labourer or footsoldier. The trials were expensive; a plaintiff had to be unusually confident or angry and afraid. One judge invoiced for £130 (which would be over £100,000 today) for his and his assistant's costs for a month's witch-hunting. This was paid by the county committee from funds garnered from Royalists and Catholics.

The most cost-effective way of dealing with witches was the ordeal by water, a practice that has gone down in folklore.[38] 'Swimming' them was supposedly illegal but King James saw it as a way of identifying those who had rejected their baptism. Suspects would have their left thumb tied to their right big toe and their right thumb tied to their left big toe. Then they would be covered in a blanket and lowered by rope into a pond or river. If they sank and drowned, they were innocent. If they stayed afloat, they were guilty. Suspects would often be dressed in several layers of baggy clothing, which trapped air and ensured a degree of buoyancy. Struggling and taking in a lungful of air would also help. Staying afloat meant that their master, the Devil, had saved them.

Hopkins was attacked by some for his witch-finding. He defended himself in a pamphlet entitled *The Discovery of Witches*. He claimed never to have taken more than 20 shillings for his duties, which was untrue. But the feeling was growing that all these witch-finders did was fleece the country of its money. Hopkins died in 1647 of the plague, though there are many stories that he met the fate that he inflicted on so many others, and was 'swum' by an angry mob. After his death, Stearne feared lawsuits as victims' families sought to overturn convictions and others tried to recover fees. Both men had been able to amass considerable fortunes from their work at a time of chaos and poverty for everyone else, when returning soldiers spread plague and the upheavals of the war had disrupted the usual workings of the country.

Sadly the death of Hopkins did not bring an end to witch persecutions in England. These continued, though not to the same extent. The approach of the European Age of Enlightenment saw certain rulers start to oppose the practice of drowning and burning witches. The Duke of Brunswick saw the dangers of these types of questioning and trial, and how suspects could be led into making the 'right' confession. He demonstrated this in front of two Jesuits who had been great witch-hunters. The Enlightenment also encouraged an opposition to organized religion, rejecting it as intellectually flawed and socially manipulative. So, witch-hunting continued at a much lower level, no longer supported in the same way by the authorities. In Leicestershire in 1760, a quarrel broke out between two old women who accused each other of witchcraft. They were swum simultaneously. One sank, the other managed to stay afloat for a short time and was pulled out by the mob, who demanded that she name and turn in her fellow evildoers. But in the end the mob grew weary of this persecution and turned on their leaders, who found themselves on trial. The public was gradually starting to see reason and tire of this folly. As Charles Mackay famously wrote, 'Men, it has been well said, think in herds; it will be seen that they go mad in herds, while they only recover their senses slowly, and one by one.'

In America it was a different story. The migration across the Atlantic had coincided with the witch craze of the early seventeenth century, and so the madness crossed over too. It is possible that many of those who left for a new life were those who were seen as different, and thus suspected or persecuted as witches (there are stories of witches being hung during the crossing, as Jonahs bringing ill fortune to the ship and its crew). It could be argued that the United

States was founded in some way on these potential scapegoats who left for a better life, free to live in the way that they wanted.

At any rate, they continued the pursuit of witches but in their own way. The 1650s was a very active period of witch-hunting in New England. Katherine Harrison, a Connecticut mother and practising fortune-teller, was accused of a variety of sins including breaking the Sabbath, lying and, best of all, being 'one who followed the army in England' – which, in other words, means a prostitute. She was subjected to numerous lawsuits and three trials for witchcraft. The Gilbert witchcraft case saw Goodwife Gilbert hung for having caused the death of Henry Stiles. Despite the obvious fact that he was shot accidentally by another man, she was deemed to have been behind this misfortune. Henry Stiles had owed money to the Gilberts and these debts were settled after his effects were sold posthumously. But the sense that something was wrong continued to linger. This death couldn't have happened solely through misadventure.

The Salem witch trials some decades later were the definitive and most awful example of transatlantic witch-hunting. They had their origins in 1691 with two local girls behaving strangely. They were joined by two more, the group all suffering from strange fits, and it became clear to the townsfolk that they had been bewitched. Various people were questioned as the processes of witch-finding began. The men questioned were invariably the husbands of the accused. In the end the community was torn apart. Twenty people were executed, over a hundred imprisoned and many more fell under suspicion. Four fifths of these were women and half the men were husbands or sons of witches. The conviction rate was much lower than it had been in Europe, however. Ironically, as the madness receded, there was an overwhelming sense that it was the trial and persecution that were Satan's handiwork, not the suspected witchcraft. He tore apart their community, looking for evidence of his own wrongdoing, and seeking to uncover and punish his acolytes (it does seem that a considerable amount of mental and moral agility would be needed to believe this). Alternatively, the witch trials were seen as God's punishment for man's sins. Elaine Showalter writes, 'Historically, witch-hunts have tended to be short. Communities decided that the trials were worse than the alleged crimes; they ran out of marginal victims and discovered malice or fraud in accusers.'

The notoriety of the Salem witch trials is in part due to

Arthur Miller's play, *The Crucible*, and how it echoes the anti-Communist witch-hunt of the McCarthy years. In his notes to the play, Miller wrote that for some it was a 'long-overdue opportunity for everyone so inclined to express publicly his guilt and sins, under the cover of accusations against the victims.' People were able to express 'long-held hatreds.' The witch-hunt's roots were political, social and economic, but it grew because 'these people had no ritual for the washing-away of sins.'

★

THE LITERAL SCAPEGOAT

Seldom has human intelligence been so wasted as when animals have been put on trial. Animals have commonly featured in sacrifices, and were used in various ways to carry away blame, in rituals such as that on the Jewish Day of Atonement and with Tyndale's scapegoat. But there were also occasions when the creatures were themselves blamed for the disaster, being promoted from expiatory victim to nominal culprit. And so they found themselves in the dock, charged with crimes entirely beyond their comprehension, in trials that resembled more a chimps' tea party than any serious judicial process.

There were two principal kinds of trial. The first was more like our own criminal trial, where an individual beast was accused of a specific offence – these have always been around and still happen today in one form or another. Animals in the service of man could be put on trial as if they were any other member of the household – horses, dogs, any domestic livestock, all could find themselves in the dock. In this respect they were given the same legal status as a human. There was an old German law that stipulated that all domestic animals should be treated as accessories to any crime committed in the house. This was at a time when superstition sometimes led people to bury a dead thief's fingers under a newly built house to protect it from theft. There are also stories of animals being put on the rack to extort confessions, though this does seem unlikely, even by the standards of the day. It would have been done to observe the proper letter of the law rather than in any actual expectation of obtaining testimony.

An animal charged with homicide would be executed just like any human.[39] In Falaise, Normandy, in 1386 a sow was charged with killing an infant, having torn its face and arms. The pig was sentenced to be 'mangled and maimed in the head and forelegs,' echoing the wounds it had inflicted on its victim, after which it was dressed in men's clothing and executed in the town square. There used to be a painting of this scene in the town church there, but it was whitewashed over in 1820; we only have an engraving of it now to remind us of this landmark in human justice. There are other cases of pigs put on trial and sentenced to be buried alive for having eaten small children – in Amiens in 1463 and in Saint-Quentin in 1557 – or burned in public, as happened in Paris in 1266.

This grotesque theatre was in some way supposed to slake the public's thirst for justice. But there was also the extraordinary idea that animals might be deterred from violence by seeing one of their own kind put to death and its corpse placed on view. This was believed by Hieronymus Rosarius, envoy to Pope Clement VII, who described how in Africa lions were crucified and placed near towns. There were also instances of wolves being hung from gallows in Germany, and, much later, an American farmer might hang a dead hawk to protect his chickens – just as modern farmers do now with crows and other birds of carrion.

This all took place at a time when animals were often seen as incarnations of demons, and so the trials might feature accusations of witchcraft. In Bâle in 1474 an old cock was put in the dock, accused of laying an egg. The prosecution alleged that Satan employed witches and demons to hatch these eggs and that the creatures that emerged, usually basilisks, would torment the human race (a cock's egg was supposed to have great magical properties; a witch would favour it over even the philosopher's stone). The defence counsel did not try to deny the fact of the egg-laying. Instead, he pleaded that no evil deed had been intended. The laying of an egg was an involuntary act and, as such, not punishable by law. He challenged the prosecution to name a single instance of the Devil having made a pact with an animal. They cited the case of the Gadarene swine, referred to in Mark's gospel, and that swung it for them. The cock was found guilty and sentenced to death as a sorcerer who'd assumed the shape of a bird. He and the egg were burned together at the stake.

As if this was not enough, animals could also be punished for having a crime committed against them. Often, if a man was successfully prosecuted for bestiality, then both he and the object of his affections would be burned. There was a case of this in Paris, living up its reputation as the city of lovers, in 1546, involving a man and a cow who were hanged and then burned. The same tribunal had convicted a man and a sow 80 years previously. In 1662 in New Haven, a 60-year-old man was executed for bestiality along with his cow, two heifers, two sows and three sheep – a story that is crying out to be immortalized in a nursery rhyme, along the lines of 'The Twelve Days of Christmas'. This man was also a great lover of dogs and began with them aged 10, allegedly, before moving on to pastures new. But no amount of human guilt could save the animals from sharing the fate of their tormentor. After these trials it was standard procedure for the guilty party to compensate the owner of the animal for their loss; in fact it was law, one that came from the Bible, from the Books of Exodus and Leviticus. Incidentally, when burning the bodies, the man's would be placed under those of the beasts.

Fortunately, it seems that reason gradually returned, to France at least. In 1750, when a man named Jacques Ferron was caught *in flagrante* with a she-ass, he was sentenced to death, but the she-ass walked free. She was acquitted as a victim of violence and an unwilling participant, and many came forward to testify to her previously good character, including the prior of the local convent.

It was not just the French who put unwitting perpetrators on trial. Other countries had similar practices, including charging corpses for crimes they had committed in life. In Shanghai in 1888, a Chinese salt smuggler was convicted and beheaded, having already died some time before. Closer to home, when Stephen VI became pope in 896 one of his first acts was to have the body of his predecessor Formosus exhumed and put on trial for having behaved unlawfully and disgracing the papacy. All legal formalities were used in the trial of this eight-month-old corpse, which was dressed up in full papal splendour. A deacon was appointed to defend him, though a guilty verdict was always going to be brought in. When the dead ex-pope was found guilty his benedictory fingers were cut off and his body stripped, then dragged to and dumped in the Tiber. Months later, when Stephen himself had been strangled in prison, Formosus' mutilated, rotting remains were restored to his tomb.

This obsession with finding a culprit could extend to inanimate objects. In Russia, after a prince was assassinated in the town of Uglich in 1591, the bell sounded the signal of insurrection and, for this serious offence, it was transported to Siberia along with the humans who had been banished in the more traditional way. The bell was not pardoned and restored to Uglich until 1892.

The Ancient Greeks also prosecuted lifeless objects, should these have caused someone's death. For instance, a statue that fell and crushed a man, or a sword used by a murderer would each be publicly condemned and removed and placed outside the city's boundaries. Plato drew up a law to deal with such cases. If a beast killed a man it should be prosecuted and driven outside the city's limits, and likewise a lifeless object, unless it was a thunderbolt hurled by one of the gods. None of this was intended as a way of preventing further tragedies (whereas torturing a pig in public was clearly, in some demented way, supposed to do that by sending a clear message to its fellow creatures); rather it was a ceremony used to make sense of the tragedy. The Greeks and medieval Europeans both suffered from the fear that they lived in a lawless world and these rituals were a way of coping with disaster and answering that eternally nagging question, 'If there is a god, why does he let these things happen to us?' The Greeks believed that if a murder was not properly atoned for, the Furies would be summoned and they would bring pestilence to the land. This was the case whether the crime was committed by man or beast.

As well as seeking atonement, these trials tried to make sense of the universe by taking certain terrible, inexplicable events and redefining them as crimes. Society could cope with wickedness, and had a system in place for dealing with it, but struggled in the face of random adversity.

The animal trials of individual beasts tended to be secular affairs but when whole groups of animals were responsible the Church was brought in. Insects and rodents were not seen as subject to human control in the same way as domestic animals and so they were designated differently, requiring supernatural control, which meant priests. So, farmers whose crops were being ravaged by insects or other pests would appeal to their local cleric for assistance in dealing with these public nuisances.

This assistance could come in a variety of forms. Initially the Church would provide 'metaphysical aid', expelling the creatures with prayer, processions and exorcisms, all helped along with gallons of holy water. In Füssen in Bavaria, the crosier of St. Magnus was kept. This was solemnly borne aloft as a way of dealing with infestations of mice, rats and insects. But many things could go wrong, and these interventions were not always successful. The priests would have to be word perfect when it came to reciting the incantations to drive the insects away. One stumble or mistake and the whole thing wouldn't work. Here we see the importance of ritual. The need for precision was a way of explaining the instances when it didn't work. Something must have been wrong in the execution rather than the whole concept of metaphysical aid being flawed. The spells might also not work if the local congregation had not paid their tithes promptly enough, and, as always, any excessively sinful behaviour could be the reason. It would always be the sins of the masses, rather than the élite, that caused the tragedy (I have been searching in vain for an instance of a leader claiming that a disaster was visited upon his people as punishment for his own sins).

More extreme methods of dealing with infestations could be resorted to. One of these was instant excommunication. There are many stories of holy men driving out pests. St. Bernard was said to have excommunicated a swarm of flies that was annoying the congregation of the abbey church of Forigny. The swarm died the very next day, falling immediately to the floor and having to be cleared out with shovels, 'all dead corpses', according to the Abbot of St. Theodore in Rheims. A more secular account shows a deplorable lack of imagination in mentioning a very sharp overnight frost. St. Eldrad had commanded snakes to leave the valley of Briançon, just as St. Patrick is credited with having driven them out of Ireland. Maybe the snake, alone of God's creatures, had no rights, after all it was held responsible for man's expulsion from Eden. And in the sixteenth century giant sea creatures, known as *terones*, were excommunicated after getting caught in fishermen's nets, destroying them in the process.

Excommunication tended to happen with more severe

cases. In the Tyrol in 1338, a swarm of locusts began to devastate the crops, laying eggs and showing no signs of leaving. Usually, locusts would depart once they'd eaten every bit of greenery and brought the inhabitants there to the brink of starvation. This time, a prosecution was launched against them in the ecclesiastical court of Kaltern, a nearby town. The priest there excommunicated the locusts 'in the name of the Blessed Trinity, Father, Son and Holy Ghost'. In the ninth century, the area around Rome was plagued with swarms of locusts. A reward was offered for their extermination but they survived the peasants' efforts to wipe them out. Pope Stephen VI had great quantities of holy water prepared and the countryside was sprinkled with it, and, sure enough, that worked. There were other similar cases in Mantua and Lombardy with locusts 'as long as a man's finger, with large heads and bellies filled with vileness; and when dead they infected the air and gave forth a stench, which even carrion kites and carnivorous beasts could not endure.' In a case in Tartary the locusts were supposed to have blocked out the sun and covered the ground a cubit deep.

On the whole, it was frowned upon to expel animals without due process. So, if the prayers and processions didn't work (owing to human failure, obviously), then there would in time be a court case. These would differ greatly from the trials of individual animals. Not only were these trials of rodents and insects mostly dealt with by ecclesiastical courts, but they were civil suits rather than penal prosecutions. They were prosecuting the vermin for the damage done to the possessions of others, usually the harvest and fruits of the field. Though in this they were really technically incorrect, being prohibitive actions, rather than ones aimed at recovering compensation for the victims. After all, insects don't have any material wealth, and the Church was not going to reach into its coffers to compensate the congregation.

The Church could not quite work out what stance to take on animals. The scholar Origen asked if beasts were a species of man or man a species of beast. Both ideas were incompatible with the teachings of Christianity, he felt. The only way of making sense of it all was to propose the theory that animals were incarnations of evil spirits. In the case of insects, some agreed with him and felt they were sent by Satan, being demons working for him. Others saw them as creatures of God, who'd come to punish us on his orders. It would be sacrilegious to impede his work.

Each case was treated differently. If it was felt that the pests were sent by Satan, they should be cast out, into the sea for example, where they would die. If they were sent by God, then they should be driven out somewhere pleasant and set aside for them, so man and beast could co-exist happily, without damage to the former's crops. Obviously, it was not always easy to distinguish between the two. Another factor for the court to consider was the status of the animal on trial. Should they be treated as a lay person or as a member of the clergy? For instance, a *clerus* beetle might be seen as the latter, but most creatures were the former. *Le Livre du Roy Modus et de la Reyne Racio* (1486) divides animals into two categories – those of *bestes doulces* and *bestes puantes*. Doves and deer fall into the former group; pigs, wolves, foxes and ravens into the latter. This split is mirrored in many other cultures, between those creatures supposed to be noble and pure, and those that are more susceptible to possession by evil spirits. Insects were felt to be especially dangerous, being both easily possessed and more easily swallowed by unwitting victims. And the majority of these court cases were against insects.

There was a case in 1478 in Switzerland involving an insect known as the inger, which was devastating the local crops. The bishop of Lausanne presided over the trial, as the mayor and council of Berne sought to rid themselves of this menace. The parish priest began by issuing a prayer of warning to the inger:

> Thou irrational and imperfect creature, the inger, called imperfect because there was none of thy species in Noah's ark at the time of the great bane and ruin of the deluge.

The insects were told

> to depart within the next six days from all places where you have secretly or openly done or might still do damage, also to depart from all fields, meadows, gardens, pastures, trees, herbs, and spots, where things nutritious to men and to beasts spring up and grow, and to betake yourselves to the spots and places, where you and your bands shall not be able to do any harm secretly or openly to the fruits and aliments nourishing to men and beasts.

The inger were summoned to appear at a certain date in Wifflisburg to answer for their conduct. There is no further record of this having taken place, and another trial took place the following year. The commune proceeded to charge and burden [the inger] with our curse, and command them to be obedient and anthematize them in the name of the Father, the Son and the Holy Ghost, that they turn away from all fields, grounds, enclosures, seeds, fruits and produce, and depart. By the same sentence I declare and affirm that you are banned and exorcised, and through the power of Almighty God shall be called accursed and shall daily decrease whithersoever you may go, to the end that of you nothing shall remain save for the use and profit of man.

And that is how to excommunicate an insect. But it didn't always go that far.

In 1545, the wine-growers of St Julien launched legal proceedings against an infestation of weevils that was devastating their vines. Initially the Church advocated a round of public prayers, having discussed the case and decided that God put vegetation on earth for both man and beast to enjoy. For that reason it would be unseemly to take any hasty or extreme course of action against the weevils. The growers and the rest of the population were asked to beg for forgiveness for their sins and, most importantly, to pay their tithes on time. Several masses were held and the host was carried with great solemnity around the vineyards. At least two members of each household were invited to participate in this charade and, after a while, the insects disappeared. Once again, the Church had demonstrated the breadth of its powers, as a sixteenth-century forerunner of Rentokil.

Thirty years later the weevils returned and in time they were brought to trial. The prosecution sought to have the insects excommunicated. The defence cited verses from Genesis as a reason for not doing so. The prosecution countered that though animals were created before man it was intended by God that they should be subordinate to him and for this reason they were created first. The defence argued that being subordinate did not automatically entail being excommunicated, and debate raged on. In the end a piece of land was set aside for the weevils to occupy. It was decided that the inhabitants of St Julien were entitled to pass through this land and use the water there. Any mining rights were also theirs. Otherwise the weevils should be free to do as they wished with it. This, however, did not mean an end to the litigation. The prosecution had made it clear that they regarded this as an extremely generous offer and that the weevils should forthwith cease their destructive ways and leave the vineyards, never to return, on pain of excommunication.

The weevils blithely continued their existence, unaware of these goings-on. And so the prosecution and defence found themselves in court again. The latter stood up and claimed that the specified land was not suitable for his clients, not being fertile enough for their needs. The prosecution shrieked that it was admirably suited for them, having plenty of trees and shrubs of various kinds. The court decided that an expert should examine the site and submit a written report of its suitability as a refuge for the insects. For this the expert was paid 3 florins, while 16 went towards clerical work. The vicar received 3. I would love to relate how this nonsense all ended but history has dealt with it in a much more appropriate way, the final page of the court records having been destroyed by insects of some kind – perhaps even the defendants themselves.

This trial lasted eight months, though that was in part due to the military activity of the time, which kept delaying proceedings, as the Duke of Savoy readied his army for an invasion. Two things emerge from this trial – that it was believed that the insects had a right to sustenance, and that the Church had the power to make them stop their ravages, even force them to move elsewhere. There was total faith in the Church's power to do this; otherwise, of course, the trial would have been a farce. A third factor emerges from this case – the length of time over which it unfolded. The more the Church could spin out proceedings, the more likely that Mother Earth would play its part and bring about a natural end to everything. The insects might die from a change in climate, or just move on – and the Church would take credit.

But let us look at precisely how these sorts of proceedings were spun out. Bartholomew Chassenée was a very distinguished French jurist of the sixteenth century. He made his name defending some rats accused of destroying a barley crop. The day of the trial came and there was no sign of his clients. He successfully argued that since they were scattered all over the place, a single summons would not serve to gather them all. And so a second summons was published from the pulpits of places that were known to be infested with rats. After that, and when they still did not appear, he claimed that the absence of his clients was really due to the length and difficulty of the journey that faced them. After all, they would have been at great risk from their ever-vigilant enemy, the cats. Since it was impossible to guarantee their safety, they could not attend to face the charges against them. Another similar case happened in Stelvio, in Western Tyrol, when the commune launched legal proceedings against some field mice. The counsel for the defence requested formal protection for his clients from cats and dogs, to ensure their safe passage.

These trials would proceed with great formality and ingenuity, and an extraordinary range of literary references and allusions. First would come the *requeste des habitans*, followed by the *plaidoyer des habitans*, then the *réplique du défendeur*, the *conclusions du procureur Episcopal* and finally the *sentence du juge d'église*. Quotations would be scattered liberally from an extraordinary range of works, many in Latin and few of any relevance at all, with plenty of classical allusions too – what Milton called a 'horseload of citations'. All of this in a desperate attempt to lend gravitas to the absurd theatre of it all.

For instance, in one trial, the prosecution quoted the likes of Pliny, Paul, Moses and Ovid in his reply, citing numerous precedents of holy men excommunicating animals. In Aix, St. Hugon, the bishop of Grenoble, excommunicated the serpents who infested the warm baths there. Afterwards, it is said, the snakes did not kill with their bite, their venom having been drawn by the intervention. The Bible, and Genesis in particular, was consulted frequently in an attempt to make sense of it all. The following lines were usually quoted as the official line on the rights of animals: 'And to every beast of the earth, and to every fowl of the air, and to everything that creepeth upon the earth, wherein there is life, I have given every green herb for meat: and it was so' (Genesis 1:30). Also, 'I will also send wild beasts among you, which shall rob you of your children, and destroy your cattle, and make you few in number; and your high ways shall be desolate' (Leviticus 26:22).

But the following questions were left unanswered, being in fact unanswerable. Did animals have rights, just as man does, to the fruits of nature? Do they have souls and free will? Could they be excommunicated? All these conundrums were leapt on by skilful defence counsels, along with the smallest inconsistency of procedure, to acquit their clients.

Animals were tried by ecclesiastical courts which could only impose canonical sentences. And, as with witches and heretics, so it was for beetles and bunnies – once it had been decreed that they should die, it was left to a secular court to make the formal condemnation, while the Church made a hollow plea for mercy (even in its dirtiest moments, the Church liked to pretend its hands were clean).

Ironically, animal interaction does not appear so different from our own blaming behaviour. There are hierarchies everywhere in nature, from bumble bees to chickens. The Norwegian zoologist Thorleif Schjelderup-Ebbe noticed this first in hens. Even when starving, hens would let the dominant bird in the flock eat before them, waiting until it had finished before feeding themselves. This process would continue all the way down the pecking order, until you reached the hens right at the bottom. These obviously got less to eat, had fewer offspring and suffered from severe stress and physical ailments. Often, in times of extreme need and chaos – caused by famine and overpopulation – these birds would be attacked and scapegoated. They paid the price for the stability of the group, and this structure ensured less fighting and increased the production of eggs. These same attributes have been observed in other creatures (including ourselves, obviously).

At the end of E.P. Evans' book, *The Criminal Prosecution and Capital Punishment of Animals*, he includes a list of animals that were prosecuted and excommunicated. Even at half the length, the list would be a fine testimony to human credulity, stupidity and cruelty. It includes moles, locusts, snakes, field mice, caterpillars, flies, eels, pigs, bulls, horses, rats, cows, weevils, cocks, snails, worms, beetles, dogs, asses, grasshoppers, sheep, dolphins, turtle doves, termites, wolves, and, fittingly enough, a he-goat, who was banished to Siberia.

THE COMMUNIST
SCAPEGOAT

'The whole aim of practical politics is to keep the populace alarmed by menacing it with an endless series of hobgoblins, all of them imaginary. Criminals, immigrants, certain states, all used to conceal the failure of the system to look after its people.'

H. L. Mencken

The twentieth century brought a new dimension to the practice of scapegoating. Totalitarian regimes moved it up a gear; the self-styled perfect form of government could not be seen to brook any form of failure, and so it apportioned blame with extraordinary ferocity. They used propaganda to create an enemy, demonizing them in the way the Catholic Church had its foes centuries before, creating the idea of this shadowy force responsible for every mishap. The first major example of this happened as a result of the Russian Revolution. Lenin was convinced that the enemy should be destroyed, not just defeated. Enemies of the State should be put on trial, individuals should be found and blamed for the people's misfortunes. Scapegoating was the most effective way of discrediting the enemy completely, of eliminating any challenge to authority. This strategy would endure in Communist thinking.

By 1937 the Soviet Union was in terrible shape after war, civil war and immense social change, which had been brought about with brutality. The peasants had been forcibly collectivized, millions had been dispersed and millions had starved. This great social experiment had propelled to power many who had no real experience of leadership, and the effects were truly awful. But someone else needed to be blamed for all this misery. It couldn't be seen to be the totalitarian impulse to perfect and remodel humanity that had caused this – rather there had to be a giant conspiracy to blame.

The Moscow show trials of the late 1930s were designed to drive this message home publicly while also removing any potential challenges to Stalin's rule. On 23 January 1937, 17 high-ranking members of the Communist Party confessed to having plotted with Soviet enemies (in this instance, the Nazi Party) to undermine the Soviet state on Leon Trotsky's orders, committing numerous acts of sabotage. There had been trials the year before, and more followed. By the time they ended, almost every surviving member of Lenin's Politburo had been put on trial.

In these trials Trotsky found himself blamed for most Soviet ills. He and Stalin had plotted against each other for years, but it was not until Trotsky denounced Stalin as the gravedigger of the Revolution that he was doomed. He was exiled a year afterwards, and from that moment on was the scapegoat for all Soviet problems, although oddly he was driven out before being blamed (this is echoed in George Orwell's *Animal Farm*, where the former leader Snowball is driven out from the community and subsequently held responsible for all that goes wrong).

In July 1936, the Central Committee had issued the following proclamation:

> The indelible mark of every Bolshevik in the current situation ought to be his ability to recognize and iden-tify enemies of the party no matter how well they may have camouflaged their identity.

As in the witch crazes hundreds of years previously, it was prudent to see every accident and example of incompetence as a malign act. And as with the witch trials, the accused often collaborated with their accusers, even confessing to more than they were accused of. Why would they do this? It was not just a reaction to the brutality of their treatment and the threats against their families, but in some cases it was a final act of loyalty from old Bolsheviks. Through their confessions they could continue the pretence that the evil affecting Russia was not endemic in the system, but rather was something external.

The Moscow show trials had been preceded by 'warm-up' trials, which had resulted from a series of industrial accidents. In 1928 over 50 Russian and foreign engineers were put in the dock, accused of having blown up mines near Shakhty. Eleven of them were sentenced to death, five actually being executed. Two years later the Industrial Party trial took place. It maintained that a secret organization existed, supported by foreign elements and that its aim was the overthrow of Communism. But it was only after the assassination of Kirov in 1934 that the former Bolshevik leadership found itself linked to this plot and held to account. Kirov's assassin, Nikolayev, claimed that Trotsky had in part financed the conspiracy.

The question of whether the leadership really was as paranoid as these cases would suggest needs to be asked. Or were these trials cynical measures to assuage the misery of the masses and remove any challenges to Stalin's authority? As with all scapegoating, these trials encouraged the positive belief that the great problems affecting society could be solved by ridding it of the evil-doers. It was easier to think this way than to believe the worst. The idea that the authorities did not know what they were doing was too terrible to bear for those who'd suffered so much.

After the Second World War, the Russians brought the expertise they'd acquired from their show trials to Nuremberg. The impetus for these postwar trials came entirely from them; Churchill and Roosevelt had wanted to shoot the Nazi leadership instead. But the Soviets wanted formal retribution. War crimes trials such as those at Nuremberg were a feature of the second half of the twentieth century, from that of Slobodan Milosevic to Saddam Hussein. There were equivalent trials after the Second World War in Tokyo, although Emperor Hirohito was spared this process, the Allies not being intent on the destruction of his regime.

This Soviet style of prosecuting the Nazis was echoed in the West. In America the House Un-American Activities Committee was formed in May 1938, ostensibly to fight the Nazi menace, but it soon decided that the Communists were more dangerous. Many organizations were designated as suspicious, including 438 newspapers, 280 unions and the Boy Scouts. During the Second World War the anti-Soviet focus waned, as the US found itself supplying the USSR with arms and supplies. But after the war, the fear of the Red threat re-emerged. In Hollywood, directors, actors and producers were all questioned about possible Communist sympathies. Cinema was seen as such a powerful medium, much more so than other art forms, that the greatest vigilance was required. When China became Communist in 1949 the panic grew. Only months earlier Russia had successfully tested an atom bomb. It was now that Senator Joseph McCarthy mounted his anti-Communist crusade, seeing their malign influence everywhere. He and others believed that every Communist power acted as one under the orders of the Russian leadership. Barbara Tuchman wrote in *The March of Folly*:

The witch-hunts of McCarthyism, of the House Un-American Activities Committee, the informers, the blacklists and the fire-eaters of the Republican right and the China lobby, the trail of wrecked careers, had plunged the country into a fit of moral cowardice. Even Dulles apparently trembled at the thought that the McCarthy onslaught might one day turn on him.

The Rosenbergs were executed for passing nuclear secrets to the Communists, leaving two children as orphans. But by 1954 the Red Scare started to die down and McCarthy was no longer heeded in quite the same way. The fact is that his theories did not hold water – America had actually prospered and become much more powerful during this time.

THE FINANCIAL
SCAPEGOAT

There are a few catastrophes that affect almost everyone, and economic collapse is foremost among these. The more materialistic a society is, the more economic trouble hurts. The triggers for these collapses are extraordinarily complex and hard to fathom, yet that does not deter the blamemongers. Every disaster must have its scapegoat, and the world of finance is no exception. On the whole, though, it blames those within its system – either those who lost or spent all the money, or those who took it.

Economic disaster tends to be blamed on a rogue financier or two. Nick Leeson was accused of bringing down Barings, incurring huge losses through wild, unauthorized trading; likewise Jérôme Kerviel was accused of losing 4.9 billion Euros while working for Société Générale.[40] More recently, individuals like Fred Goodwin have been accused of causing the current recession. But really these were not the only bad apples – rather the barrel was rotten. As we have already seen by concentrating on the individual, an overhaul of the corrupt system is avoided.

The City has always been densely populated with likely candidates, financiers commanding little sympathy from the public, on the whole. Few understand quite what they do and why they get paid so much for it. The central conceit of Tom Wolfe's *Bonfire of the Vanities* is that Sherman McCoy – 'Master of the Universe ... salary like a telephone number' – is unable to explain to his young daughter quite what he does for a living. Protected behind a barrier of jargon, of hedges, derivatives and other financial instruments, the City is not unlike the Catholic Church of the Middle Ages (though there is no pope and certainly no infallibility).

These bankers might be essential to the economy, keeping the flow of money moving, but they are regarded by the public as being grossly overpaid. After all, sewage workers and IT professionals perform essential roles in other areas of our lives, yet are not remunerated in the same way. But ultimately those who direct the flow of money around our economy are always going to ensure a large amount of it flows towards them. In any case, a backlash was overdue.

History has seen this before. Firstly, there is the collapse of a bubble – when an asset has become valued far higher than can be justified by its future returns. People are buying these assets in the knowledge that someone else will immediately buy them for a higher price – the law of the 'greater fool'. There have been numerous examples of these bubbles. The South Sea Bubble in Britain saw a group of merchantmen buy up £9 million of the British government's debt, assured of an interest rate of 6 per cent annually. These merchants were known as the South Sea Trading Company and they had obtained exclusive trading rights to several South American ports. Fuelled by wild rumours of the fortunes that were to be made on that continent, stock in the South Sea Trading Company rose unprecedentedly in 1720 as everyone rushed to invest. Overnight other trading companies were set up to take advantage of this mania, most famously, 'A company for carrying on an undertaking of great advantage, but nobody to know what it is.' The founder of this one saw his office besieged. After five hours of trading he had made 2,000 livres, whereupon he packed up, left for the Continent and was never heard of again. Other rival schemes mostly dealt with trading in gold, but there was one that focused on hair, and another on a wheel of perpetual motion. When these all collapsed, the government (having endorsed the whole affair) was swift to blame the wicked merchants, most of whom had fled with their gains. But really, this was a situation where all sides were to blame. Faced with the prospect of free money, everyone lost their way.

In France, similar havoc occurred with the Mississippi Company. Louis XIV died in 1715, having only ever been praised during his lifetime. After his death, he was vilified for his financial profligacy after leaving France in economic chaos. A Scottish economist, John Law, was appointed the nation's Controller General of Finances and set up the Mississippi Company. This too was a scheme for trading with the New World (in this case Louisiana). Law had wildly exaggerated the area's wealth, and the French public duly invested in his scheme, but it foundered under the hysteria. In *Extraordinary Popular Delusions and the Madness of Crowds*, Charles Mackay describes how Law was blamed for the crowd's folly – he was the boatman dashed to pieces on the rocks as 'the waters maddened and turned to foam by the rough descent, only boiled and bubbled for a time, and then flowed on as smoothly as ever.' Law was held accountable for the scheme's demise and dismissed from his post by the Regent who had appointed him in the first place. He fled from France, leaving behind his wealth, though he had not personally enriched himself through his scheme, which was devised as a way of rescuing France from its debt.

The most notorious bubble was the Dutch tulip fever. Here the Dutch rushed to invest their money in tulip bulbs, convinced that this would lead to great wealth. As a result the bulbs became stupendously overvalued. Mackay claims that people were selling their houses and investing the proceeds in bulbs. A Dutch sailor was supposed to have eaten one, mistaking it for an onion, and for this he was thrown in prison. When the tulip market crashed, 'the cry of distress resounded everywhere and each man accused his neighbour.'

These bubbles generally tended not to produce scapegoats in quite the way that other financial disasters did. Those who were seen to profit from the collapse would be vilified and targeted, as we do with short sellers today, for instance. But on the whole the crowd is dimly aware at some level of its stupidity, and most of those who profited tremendously from these bubbles had the good sense either not to stick around or to conceal their gains. Other financial crises differ in this respect.

The economic mismanagement that led to the devaluation of Germany's currency during the Weimar

Republic, discussed later, was crucial in the rise of the Nazi Party. But the crisis of monetary devaluation is not just a modern phenomenon. In 1404 an Act of Parliament was passed banning the manufacture of gold and silver. Even then they understood the dangers of devaluing currency, and what disaster a medieval alchemist might cause should he successfully turn lead into gold. Many early crises were caused by rulers reducing the silver or gold content in their coinage to cope with budget deficits caused by the need to spend money on wars. Dionysius of Syracuse in fourth-century BC Greece was one of the first monarchs in history to default on his debt. He had borrowed from his subjects, giving them promissory notes in exchange. He subsequently decreed that all money in circulation should be turned over to his government upon pain of death. Each one-drachma coin was subsequently restamped to make it into a two-drachma coin before he repaid his subjects, creating a 100 per cent rate of inflation in the process.

Henry VIII was almost as profligate with his currency as he was with his wives. He had inherited an enormous fortune from Henry VII, confiscated much of the Church's land and wealth and yet still had to debase the currency by clipping coins. Over the years from 1542 to the end of his reign in 1547 the pound lost 83 per cent of its value. The creation of paper money made this kind of devaluation even easier. In *This Time Is Different: Eight Centuries of Financial Folly*, Carmen M. Reinhart and Kenneth S. Rogoff wonder if Latin America might not have found financial stability easier to come by had the printing press not crossed the Atlantic.

Weimar Germany saw the most famous case of the devaluation of a currency after the First World War. The expression 'wheelbarrow inflation' was coined, as the government printed never-ending numbers of bank notes of spiralling value; famously, wheelbarrowfuls of the old small-denomination notes were required just to buy a loaf of bread. By late 1923 the government was issuing one-hundred-trillion-mark bank notes, and the dollar was worth four trillion marks. Suddenly the nation's money was no longer its own, and each month brought new levels of difficulty to daily life. Theft, prostitution and corruption thrived as everyone tried to stave off financial ruin. The prime minister of Bavaria even submitted a bill aiming to make gluttony a criminal offence.

In this climate, everyone was looking for someone to blame. Germany had been made to pay reparations as penance for having started the First World War, and this was held responsible in part for the financial difficulty the country found itself in. But there was more to it than that. Great hatred began to be directed at those who were thought to have profited from both the war and the ensuing economic chaos. And this swung towards financial speculators and the Jews.

It is well documented how extreme Hitler's views first seemed, as he denounced everyone and everything. But as life became much harder, people started to listen to him, even to think he might be right. He traded on a semi-dormant hatred of the Jews; 18 centuries of stereotyping them in a negative way lent considerable weight to his attempts to dehumanize them. As he himself wrote, 'The art of all truly great national leaders consists among other things primarily in not dividing the attention of a people, but in concentrating it on a great foe.' This thinking would lead to the Holocaust. Hitler sought to create a perfect world, a world without scapegoats – by purging it of them. In the utopia he envisaged, there would be no need to blame.

THE MEDICAL
SCAPEGOAT

Every outbreak of a disease has a Patient Zero or index case – the first person to confirm the existence of the outbreak. Unsurprisingly, this individual can sometimes become the focus of blame for the plague, particularly in the modern era. The term Patient Zero was coined after the spread of HIV in North America and was attached to a Canadian air steward, Gaëtan Dugas. He had had a number of sexual partners whom he'd infected with the virus, which spread further through them. For this he was vilified, accused of passing on HIV knowingly to thousands of partners. But he is just one person in a long tradition of blaming a complex frightening illness on an individual or group.

In the ancient world hospitals were for the poor and orphaned, where the sick and insane were looked after by widows and fallen women. They were intended as quarantines as much as places of healing. Illness was once seen as a punishment for sin, usually sent by the gods. This belief originated with the Assyrians and has been adopted by almost every society since. Even in the West today, we convince ourselves that by leading the right – even moral – life, we can avoid illness. And so when a disease strikes, people can't help but consider what sin brought it, almost as naturally as they are looking for the cure.

When the Black Death hit Europe in the fourteenth century, in many instances it was blamed on the Jews, who were accused of spreading the disease and poisoning the water system. From 1348 to 1351 over 200 Jewish communities were exterminated in Germany. In Erfurt there is evidence of an uprising against the Jews at the time that the plague struck, when between 100 and 1,000 people were killed. The Erfurt Treasure (which is now in the Yeshiva University Museum in Manhattan) was buried around 1349. A chest, containing hundreds of items of gold jewellery and thousands of silver coins, was hidden by its Jewish owners who clearly fled the town hoping to return and collect their treasure at a later date. But they never did, and it stayed in the ground until 1998.

This was part of a long history of general persecution of the Jews. One theory as to why they were blamed for the plague at this time is that it tended to spare them. The outbreak peaked in spring, around Passover, when grain would have been removed from Jewish households. This would have led to fewer rats there, so limiting the spread of the plague.

The plague was not solely blamed on the Jews, however. The Sultan of Cairo decreed that the plague was a divine judgement for the sin of fornication, and therefore women were to blame. He banned them from going outside. In Britain the Bishop of Winchester blamed man's sensuality and organized thrice-weekly barefoot processions. His diocese was harder hit than any other, these processions no doubt having contributed to the spread of the disease. The Flagellants scourged themselves even harder with whips to avert God's anger, but likewise, their travelling ways would only have worsened matters. Some held cats responsible and killed them, again worsening matters as rat numbers grew and carried the disease further afield. And it could be argued that Pope Boniface was in part responsible. His Bull of 1300 had banned the mutilation of corpses, thus outlawing the anatomical dissection of bodies. Medicine suffered accordingly, and, when the plague struck, doctors were helpless (the medical faculty of the University of Paris declared the Black Death to be the result of the meeting of the influences of Mars, Saturn and Jupiter).

It is not known precisely how the plague arrived in

Europe – whether it was brought by the Mongol hordes, or Indian or Egyptian sailors, who brought the black rats with them. Most human diseases do come from animals. Occasionally it makes sense to cull them, to prevent the further spread of the outbreak, but most often these creatures are punished needlessly. Killing them gives the impression of action. But really, most outbreaks are so complex that there is rarely a single factor and this form of blame achieves nothing.

The first outbreak of what became known as the Black Death was the Plague of Justinian, which hit the Roman Empire in the sixth century AD and returned again some decades later. The estimated death toll was 25 million. It was named after the emperor of the time of its arrival; he himself contracted the plague, but survived it. Previously Rome had been struck by the Antonine Plague, which killed millions of Roman citizens between AD 165 and 180. At its height, 5,000 were dying of it every day. Soldiers returning from successful campaigns brought the disease back, and the expansion of world trade routes in Roman times also contributed to its spread. Antoninus was one of two Emperors killed by it, and so gave his name to the outbreak.

The naming of diseases provides us with the most

obvious form of scapegoating.[41] Spanish Flu is a prominent example of this, leading to an indelible ethnic association and so a form of demonization. The 1918 outbreak of Spanish Flu should really have been known as the Kansas Flu. The first identifiable cases have been traced there, though others have speculated that it began in Austria or in the Far East. At any rate, the outbreak did not originate in Spain; instead it crossed the Atlantic on troop ships and was only reported in Spain which, not being at war, did not censor reports of the disease.

The process of naming a disease after a place has sometimes been more deliberately malicious. Syphilis, for example, has been known by names that served to demonize another nation. So it would be known as the French disease in Italy and as the Italian disease in France.

THE CONSPIRACY
THEORY

'The Rosicrucians were everywhere, aided by
the fact they didn't exist.'
Umberto Eco, *Foucault's Pendulum*

The idea that forces of evil conspire against us has always had tremendous popular appeal. These conspiracy theories flourish more than ever in the age of the internet. They are a variation on the idea of scapegoating, but always involve more than one figure of blame. There is never just the lone gunman but always an organization behind him, orchestrating the chaos. There are no accidents, only evil intent, and a truly formidable enemy. It is a strangely comforting view for many. As H. L. Mencken wrote,

the central belief of every moron is that he is the victim of a mysterious conspiracy against his common rights and true deserts ... [He] ascribes all his failures to get on in the world, all his congenital incapacity and

167

damnfoolishness, to the machinations of werewolves assembled in Wall Street, or some other such den of infamy.

There are those who blame beings stranger than werewolves. David Icke, a former professional footballer[42] turned author and lecturer, is convinced that the world is run by a secret cabal of giant shape-shifting extraterrestrial lizards known as the Babylonian Brotherhood (it is unclear how these are related to their fellow reptile, the serpent in Genesis). These lizards practise ritual child sacrifice, drink blood, worship owls and number many former US presidents in their ranks including both George Bushes, as well as Kris Kristofferson and Boxcar Willie. The British royal family is also well represented – the late Queen Mother was one of these reptilian aliens, as is Prince Philip, apparently. This brotherhood is responsible for controlling many of the world's institutions, from the United Nations and the Bilderberg Group to the media and the internet. Their goal is world domination and for us all to be microchipped.

Icke once proclaimed himself the Son of God on the *Wogan Show*. He also predicted that the world would end in 1997. He does seem to have been wrong about the latter at least, but another great conspiracy theory emerged that year, also with Prince Philip at its centre (truly he is the modern counterpart to the *pharmakos*). The death of Princess Diana in a car crash in Paris saw an endless swirl of rumours, with the British Establishment at the centre of it. Mohamed Al Fayed sought to establish a reason for the death of his son Dodi and the Princess of Wales that ignored the most likely explanations, which were that Henri Paul was drink-driving and that no one was wearing seat belts. Al Fayed has consistently maintained that the royal family and MI6 conspired to assassinate Diana, and his outlandish ideas have garnered a surprisingly large following.

These are extreme instances of the conspiracy theory, and the majority shuns them, but they feed into more dangerous and mainstream ideas of racial and religious hatred. Icke is one of many believers in the authenticity of *The Protocols of the Elders of Zion* (although he denies that the giant lizards in any way symbolize the Jews). These were documents that purported to uncover a global Jewish conspiracy. They were first published in Russia in 1903 and were seized on by anti-Semites the world over – including Henry Ford – as evidence of Jewish plans for world domination. It emerged relatively quickly that *The Protocols* were a clumsy forgery and partly derived from a

French satire from the time of Napoleon III. Despite repeated debunkings (in *The Times* in 1921, and again and again afterwards) their appeal remained strong. After the First World War there was obviously a strong need to make sense of the horrors of 1914−18. For some, it became only too easy to blame the carnage entirely on the Jews. Just as some thought the Illuminati had helped bring about the French Revolution, so many preferred to blame the Jews than to recognize their own country's part in the warmongering. The re-emergence of *The Protocols* in 1919 gave this view to contemporary eyes and even Kaiser Wilhelm II, in exile in Holland, was recommending them to his guests.[43]

Although the European establishment was quick to heap scorn on *The Protocols*, there were many who clung to a belief in their veracity. The Nazis believed them to be true, as do several modern-day regimes in the Middle East. They fitted in with what people wanted to believe, and no amount of refutation could entirely dislodge these beliefs from the minds of some. Even when Henry Ford apologized publicly for 'the harm I have unintentionally committed' in supporting and publishing *The Protocols* in a newspaper he had specially set up, there were those who thought that he had merely crossed sides and joined those he opposed. Those who deny a conspiracy are inevitably perceived to be part of it.

This is partly why these stories are so resilient. Decades on, controversy still surrounds the deaths of J.F.K., Marilyn Monroe and Elvis Presley. Endless, increasingly outlandish theories about them are aired. These are then recycled in different forms, with different protagonists and victims, but the message is always the same – that a sinister other is out there, pulling the strings, and working towards our downfall. A scarcity of hard evidence is not enough to stop millions believing these theories, however. There are several explanations for this willingness to believe. David Aaronovitch sees these theories as a form of hysteria for men. Elaine Showalter agrees: 'Hysteria has not died. It has simply been relabelled for a new era … Contemporary hysterical patients blame external sources – a virus, sexual molestation, chemical warfare, satanic conspiracy, alien infiltration – for psychic problems.'

Conspiracy theories tend to first emerge from among the educated middle classes. These are people who would rather believe that there is some order in the world, even if it is an evil one. The alternative – that the world is chaotic, with no dominant being or organization above us – is too terrible to contemplate. Conspiracy theories allow us to think that we are powerful. The idea that all versions of a story are equally valid emerged with postmodernism, but in this case it's a dangerous one. Robin Ramsey, editor of the conspiracist magazine *The Lobster*, maintains that a good conspiracy theory blames the state, a bad one targets a minority. We should remember that every conspiracy theory has a victim.

There are real conspiracies, of course. Cuba is the totalitarian state whose leaders *were* right about the enemy outside their borders. The CIA really was conspiring in colourful, outlandish ways to bring down their regime. The CIA most probably did play a key role in the Iran-Contra scheme but by throwing Oliver North to the wolves they avoided any of the fallout. Nonetheless these conspiracies don't legitimize the dozens of more extreme allegations against the CIA and the other agencies responsible for national security – in particular those of attacking their own countrymen. They have been accused of assassinating J.F.K., of bringing down the Twin Towers with explosives in 2001 and of organizing the Oklahoma City bombing in 1995. But Timothy McVeigh was no scapegoat and nor were the 9/11 hijackers.

ALFRED DREYFUS

The French have provided the world with some of its leading scapegoats, most notably Alfred Dreyfus. He was entirely innocent of the crime attributed to him yet his personality and Jewishness set him apart and made him an attractive figure for blame. His case polarized national opinion for decades and had far-reaching consequences for French politics in the twentieth century. I cannot think of a more important example of a scapegoat, or a truer one, in that Dreyfus was entirely innocent of the crime imputed to him.

In the 1880s national morale in France was extraordinarily low. The French had lost Alsace to Germany after their defeat in 1870 and the era also suffered banking scandals, involving the failed attempt to build the Panama Canal. France was also a hotbed of anti-Semitism. Edouard Drumont had denounced the Jews in his bestselling book *La France Juive*, as well as having led an unsuccessful campaign against Jewish officers in the army, the French military being at the heart of the state. This was the backdrop for a series of events that would set France at loggerheads with itself, with repercussions that lasted well into the mid-twentieth century.

It all started in the German embassy in Paris when a cleaning woman found a document in the wastepaper basket and brought it back to her French masters. This *bordereau* contained military secrets that were being passed to the Germans, including information about a new piece of artillery that the French were developing. There was little evidence, but suspicion fell on a young army officer on the general staff, Alfred Dreyfus.

Dreyfus was the youngest son of a wealthy Jewish family from Alsace. His father spoke Yiddish and conducted his business in German. Dreyfus however was a great patriot, and France's defeat and loss of Alsace were personal disasters for him which shaped his whole career. He had joined the army and rose fast, becoming captain at a young age and moving to the general staff. But his Jewishness and wealth were always held against him and aroused resentment from those around him. And so he was the outsider who was the perfect suspect in this case. The evidence against him was very flimsy, largely from handwriting experts (then, an even less exact science than it is now), or it was declared too secret to be made public. He was convicted of spying for the Germans in a closed court martial, having been denied a public trial. He was subjected to a formal degradation ceremony at the École Militaire, where he was ritually stripped of his decorations and epaulettes, and had his sword broken in front of him before being sent to Devil's Island. On this remote outpost of the French empire, off the coast of South America, special conditions were imposed on him. He was imprisoned on his own, surrounded by a palisade high enough to block off the view of the sea. His captors were forbidden to speak to him, so he had no communication with anyone. At night he was chained to his bed. He was fed so badly that he was permanently malnourished and lost his teeth. But he maintained his innocence, as he would throughout his ordeal.

In France his family pursued his cause, despite a lack of evidence to support his innocence. But they slowly gained the support of many, most notably Émile Zola who would later write his famous letter, 'J'accuse', in Dreyfus' defence.[44] But behind the scenes, the authorities were finding contradictory evidence. Colonel Picquart recognized the handwriting on the *bordereau* as belonging to another officer, Esterhazy, and reported this fact to his superiors, who paid no attention. Picquart was himself both anti-Semitic and from Alsace, adding further layers to this already complex situation. Yet he pursued the issue, setting himself against the army and the French establishment.

Rumours began to circulate that Dreyfus was not guilty and that another was. Eventually Esterhazy was court-martialled, four years after the original accusation against Dreyfus. But he was protected and coached by the intelligence services throughout this process, and after two days the military judges exonerated Esterhazy in a procedure that can only be described as a whitewash. The army had no intention whatsoever of punishing the true culprit, nor of clearing the name of the wrongly imprisoned man. They couldn't afford to be wrong, having forged the documents that incriminated Dreyfus.

It was now that Zola entered the fray. His open letter to the president of the republic was published in Georges Clemenceau's liberal newspaper *L'Aurore*. In it, he accused the establishment of having punished the wrong man and of subsequently mounting a cover-up to frame him and protect the real traitor. This letter transformed the situation, wresting it from the grip of the handwriting experts and the anonymous military judges and bringing it into the open. Up until now Dreyfus had been seen as part of a Jewish conspiracy, but Zola put forward his own conspiracy theory, one that really existed. It was a revolutionary act but one for which Zola found himself on trial for defaming the army. He was convicted, and fled to London to avoid imprisonment.

Many were happy to believe in Dreyfus' guilt. After the publication of Zola's letter, thousands took to the streets, rioting and smashing the windows of Jewish-owned shops and attempting to break into synagogues. Anti-Semitic mobs demonstrated outside the courtroom in which Zola's trial was held. But the anti-Dreyfusards were not just comprised of rabid anti-Semites. Many on the left did not support Dreyfus, seeing him as their enemy – a rich, capitalist Jew.

And so the debate raged on and Dreyfus remained on Devil's Island. The president died in the arms of his mistress and in the elections that followed no one who stood could even suggest that Dreyfus might be innocent without forfeiting hundreds of thousands of votes. But the new leader did order a retrial, for which Dreyfus was brought back to France. Once more the military establishment triumphed and Dreyfus was found guilty again, this time with extenuating circumstances. If he had been declared innocent then the army would have found itself in the dock, and it was feared that they might mount a coup if that happened.

But this second guilty verdict shocked the world, for by now his case was of global interest. Both Queen Victoria and the Kaiser had declared their support for Dreyfus, Victoria describing him as a martyr. Eventually the pressure told. Dreyfus was offered a pardon, which, being in terrible health, he accepted. It was thought that he would not survive much more imprisonment. His health improved, enough even for him to fight in the French army in the First World War, where he distinguished himself. It is extraordinary that he fought for a country – and an institution – that had done so much to ruin him. But he never fully recovered from his experiences and died in 1935.

The ramifications of the Dreyfus affair were far-reaching. There was an amnesty as far as the army was concerned but the Catholic clergy found themselves punished instead by the government. In 1905 they were cut off from state support and the Church lost its role in state education, beginning its decline as it separated from the state. The anti-Dreyfus movement never went away entirely, despite his pardon. It formed Action Française and in 1940 was able to mount a successful bid for power.

It introduced more punitive statutes against the Jews than were required by the Germans, barring them from many jobs. In this way, Vichy France gradually came into existence.

THE PSYCHOLOGY OF SCAPEGOATING

*'Nothing has paralysed intelligence more than the
search for scapegoats.'*
Theodore Zeldin, *An Intimate History of Humanity*

There are many theories as to why we have this urge to blame, and all we can be certain about it is that it is an intrinsic part of our being. We used to scapegoat out of fear of divine retribution; now for the most part we do it to live with ourselves. As individuals, we create a narrative of our lives that makes sense to us, and that fits in with our concept of ourselves. Often we shape our memories accordingly. Certainly we keep some and subconsciously discard those that do not fit, demonstrating what psychologists call confirmation bias. We can find ourselves using our brains more to construct explanations and excuses once we've done what our emotions dictated, so we can pretend to ourselves that we are rational beings. But we aren't wholly rational

181

beings, as a succession of thinkers and experiments have showed.

We possess a strong self-serving bias that makes us feel special. Through this we can account for our failures and protect our sense of worth. We overrate our abilities in all sorts of ways, from intelligence to honesty. Research has shown that we all think ourselves better drivers than the norm. Likewise, we are inclined to think that we are more sensitive, loyal and in possession of a better sense of humour than others. This is particularly prevalent among men, who see themselves as 5 IQ points cleverer than they are, according to psychologist Adrian Furnham. Australians suffer from the same misplaced confidence – 86 per cent of them rate themselves as above average in their performance at work. But we cannot all be excellent drivers, or else there would be no accidents. We can't all be above average like in Garrison Keillor's fictional *Lake Wobegon* community; the laws of maths and nature ensure that some of us are below average. But we are inclined to believe that we are all special, that we're somehow different and 'it won't happen to us', leading us to take risks.

With this capacity for self-delusion it shouldn't be that much of a surprise that we seek to blame others. The idea of Attribution Theory states that we have an urgent need to find reasons for an event, and this leads us to leap to conclusions and hold others responsible. A bad situation couldn't possibly be our fault, after all. When we fail at things it is because of others; those who *are* below average bring us down. Whereas when we succeed it is due to our innate abilities (and when others succeed, we often put it down to luck).

We develop this ability to blame very early on in life. Just as children naturally express their unhappiness through tears and sobbing – designed to tell adults swiftly that something is wrong – so they, faced with the possibility of adult sanction for their actions, are quick to pass responsibility onto someone else, and quickly learn to use language to achieve this. 'He started it' is a familiar refrain in domestic life. As we move towards adulthood we should shed this defence mechanism, but really we only start to use it more.

On an everyday level we blame others to reduce cognitive dissonance – this is the state of tension that arises when we hold two contradictory ideas simultaneously (according to Plato, when desire conflicts with reason there is a disease of the soul, which is not so different from the concept of cognitive dissonance). Most of us have an innate sense of ourselves as decent people, and every bit of

183

evidence to the contrary causes us pain and discomfort. We mitigate these feelings in a variety of ways. If we admit to having behaved badly, we might excuse this behaviour by saying 'it was the drink'. We might say 'I wasn't myself'. Or we could straightforwardly blame another. In a failing relationship, couples often find themselves blaming each other for their unhappiness. With infidelity, the wronged person often finds her/himself blaming the other woman/man for their partner's betrayal, allowing them to preserve their relationship – on the surface at least. We like to personify our pain, to find one person to embody it. And so we can convince ourselves that everything would be much better if they were in our lives (as with unrequited love) or out of our lives (as with a scapegoat). But in reality it's a lot more complex than that.

Ultimately, we make scapegoats out of those we have come to believe are incapable of suffering – we dehumanize them, making them easier to hate. We create the idea that these other people are inferior to us. That develops into the idea that they therefore deserve their treatment. We deny them the same capacities for thought, emotion and values as us, and treat them accordingly. We can do this consciously or unconsciously, but the results are the same.

To see how innate this instinct is to us we can refer to Jungian psychology. Jung may not be widely followed these days but his ideas are interesting and relevant to the concept of the scapegoat. He believed that we all share the archetype of the shadow – the innate psychic structure that personifies everything we will not acknowledge about ourselves. It is the archetype of the enemy and is with us from birth; as infants we will greet our mothers with joy, while we recoil from strangers with fear and caution. We deny the existence of the shadow, and instead project its characteristics onto others, allowing us to preserve our own sense of goodness. Jung believed that there are several layers to the shadow, the top ones being unique to the individual, qualities that *he* or *she* repressed. But the bottom layer is a collective one. And it is that that has been successfully exploited in instances of mass scapegoating. By recognizing our own shadow, we make it less likely that we will project it onto others.

★

CONCLUSION

'To see what is in front of one's nose
needs a constant struggle.'
George Orwell

The only real conclusion that can be drawn from this long history is that scapegoating doesn't work. All too often it covers up the problem, rather than solving it; it focuses on rotten apples when really it is the barrel that is disintegrating around them, and it results in an incredibly harsh treatment of a minority. The most it can ever achieve is a temporary lessening of the problem, but the real roots remain. Maybe we do need some form of purification ritual, some way of allowing ourselves to forgive ourselves and move on after disaster, but this can't be it. The scapegoat is the symbol for the part of us that we most wish to remove and that society fears most at that time (witches represented lust, Jews greed and Cathars religious freedom). But removing the person does not remove that same flaw in the rest of us.

Also, there is one glaring inconsistency in the whole process. Surely if the scapegoats possessed such great powers to undermine society and trigger disaster at any point, then they should be conciliated, courted even. After all, they are able to do things that a ruler cannot. Perhaps we should even select our leaders from the ranks of the scapegoats, unless they are to be considered intrinsically evil. Ironically, perhaps the most comparable figure to the scapegoat is the hero; both give themselves up for the majority. The hero takes on risk and sacrifice, with no immediate personal advantage, and for the benefit of those around him. Is the scapegoat not just an unwilling version of this? A figure required and looked to by 'normal' society to rectify its problems?

So who is to blame, if not the scapegoat? Well, we are, of course, for most things.[45] Not for everything, although the present Bishop of Carlisle would have it otherwise – he blamed the severe flooding in Britain in 2007 on our moral degradation and the government's pro-gay legislation. This tendency is mirrored in America by the pronouncements of the American televangelist Pat Robertson, who said after the earthquake in Haiti in 2010 that the islanders had made a pact with the Devil centuries before. While many rightly choose not to listen to this, there are many who do, proving that it is after disaster that we are willing to listen to the truly lunatic, those who would rightly be ignored in all other circumstances.

So we return to the idea of stupidity. The truth is that we, who pride ourselves on being the most intelligent life-form on earth,[46] are just not quite clever enough fully to understand ourselves or the world around us. This is never more manifest than when we blame others.

I shall close with the story of a particularly hapless scapegoat. In 1666 the Great Fire of London swept through the city, burning over 13,000 houses, as well as St Paul's, 87 churches and many other prominent buildings. Famously the blaze started at Thomas Farriner's bakery in Pudding Lane in the early hours of Sunday, 2 September. Later that day the Lord Mayor, Sir Thomas Bloodworth, refused advice to demolish buildings and create fire-breaks, commenting that 'a woman could piss it out'. Fanned by high winds, the fire spread, along with wild rumours of who was to blame. Suspicion fell on the Catholics, and there were stories of an army of French and Dutch immigrants marching on London to visit further destruction upon the city.

Robert Hubert, a French apprentice watchmaker in his mid-twenties, was arrested in Romford under suspicion of trying to flee the country. He was just one of many foreigners subjected to rough treatment in the aftermath of the fire, but he rapidly confessed to arson. Initially he claimed to have thrown a fireball near the king's palace in Westminster, but he later changed this story and confessed to a litany of sins – from plotting with Frenchmen for a year to being an agent of the pope and putting a fireball through the bakery window, all for less than £5. Despite many inconsistencies and doubts over his story and sanity, Hubert was convicted and hanged at Tyburn in the middle of October. He was born a Huguenot yet died a Catholic and received the last rites. Lord Clarendon wrote afterwards that 'neither the judges nor any present at the trial did believe him guilty, but that he was a poor distracted wretch weary of his life, and chose to part with it in this way.' In fact, it soon turned out that Hubert hadn't even been in London when the fire broke out, having landed in England on 4 September. The captain of the ship testified to his complete innocence.

A monument to the fire was built near Pudding Lane, and in 1668 the following words were added to the inscription:

Here by permission of heaven, hell broke loose upon this Protestant city ... the most dreadful Burning of this City; begun and carried on by the treachery and malice of the Popish faction ... Popish frenzy which wrought such horrors, is not yet quenched ...

They remained there until 1830.

NOTES

1. Lady Grange spent eight years on the island, having been exiled there by her husband, the lord advocate of Scotland, after she spread rumours that he was a Jacobite sympathizer. She spent her time mournfully entrusting sealed letters to the sea, hoping they would reach a potential rescuer.

2. There is a superstition that relates slightly to this story – in some Scottish islands, if a fisherman drowns, the boat in which he was sailing is beached and left to rot and fall apart, being regarded as cursed. It is judged guilty of manslaughter and so must not be permitted to put to sea again, to mix with other innocent vessels. Another account of the death of the Great Auk states that the bird was washed up on the beach and found by three islanders (or two, by another account). They held it responsible for the storm, but did not put it on trial; instead they strangled it there and then. This story of the Great Auk has echoes of the Hartlepool Monkey incident. Folklore has it that a French warship was wrecked off the coast of Hartlepool during the Napoleonic Wars. The only survivor was a monkey, dressed in French uniform (presumably in its role as a mascot for the crew). The unfortunate animal was duly put on trial for being a French spy, and hanged from the mast of a fishing boat.

3. Since 1957, the British Army has had an outpost on St Kilda,

and tourists frequently visit. But there are no permanent residents.

4. Ronald Wright – *A Short History of Progress*, p.63.

5. Really Freud thought our problems stemmed from our dependence on our mothers and the resulting hostility to our fathers. Of all animals, we remain longest at the breast of our mothers, being born too soon, unready for the world.

6. For a long time, the Catholic Church shared Dr Atkins' hostility to the potato, since it was not a foodstuff that is mentioned in the Bible.

7. Another analogy is that the scapegoat is like an electrical fuse. The circuit overloads and the fuse melts, preventing a fire or other damage to the system. The fuse is replaced, and the current can continue to flow as before. The system stays as it is, and goes unrepaired. And so the situation will never resolve itself. Which is fine for everyone except for the scapegoat, who will be called upon again.

8. An example of this is the *Daily Mail*, Britain's most financially successful midmarket newspaper, with its cocktail of fear and blame. Its owners and editor have realized that blame sells, more than sex and celebrity. And so their pages are filled with villains, as well as stories nominally rooted in the science of cancer, and foods that may cause or cure it. Underlying everything is the belief that if you live the right life, bad things will not happen to you – unless someone else is to blame.

9. Here the cabinet minister is held accountable for mistakes in his/her department, whether or not he/she actually knew about them. Ultimately Carrington was responsible for employing and continuing to employ his subordinates, and thus was responsible for their actions. Though this is not enshrined in law, it is part of

the Westminster system of government. Ministers do not always take this hit, and Carrington can be seen as a more honourable example of a politician.

10. Tyndale's 'scapegoat' was a translation of the Hebrew word *azazel*, Azazel also being the standard-bearer of the rebel angels in Milton's *Paradise Lost* as well as a wilderness demon, associated with evil. The word is also derived from 'escape', meaning that Jade Goody was not so wrong when accusing her Big Brother housemates of trying to make an escape goat of her.

11. It is worth remembering that the first documents printed by Gutenberg on movable type were indulgences; these clearly took precedence over his edition of the Bible, which came second.

12. The Church's opposition to the translation of the Bible would later be echoed by American slave-owners who sought to deny their slaves access to scripture. It was made an offence to teach them to read or write.

13. I Corinthians, 3:13

14. The word tragedy comes from the Greek for 'goat song', though the derivation is not exactly clear.

15. Barbara Tuchman – *The March of Folly*, p.476.

16. Edward II and Piers Gaveston were also despised for their shared hobbies, which were not deemed aristocratic. They were both enormously fond of swimming and rowing, and Edward was also interested in blacksmithing.

17. I. A. A. Thompson – *The Institutional Background to the Rise of the Minister-Favourite*, p.19.

18. It is tempting to see this as a strong case for 'small religion' (just as there is one for small, localized government), instead of these great spiritual behemoths. But that would be to forget that

small religions either become big ones, or implode spectacularly and bloodily.

19. The theory of original sin held that a devil took hold of each child when born and so had to be exorcized through baptism. The Church believed very strongly in the practice of exorcism. A rite of exorcism should be read over the body or written down and held against the afflicted part. Catholic priests would go to work with a bell, book and candle, and there is still an official belief in the power of exorcism to this day, though the Vatican does not advertise it too widely.

20. Origen was by no means the only man to have castrated himself in Christian history. The peasant leader Kondratii Selivanor led a sect in eighteenth-century Russia which sought to purge mankind of its lust. In a misreading of key parts of the New Testament, he interpreted the word Redeemer as Castrator, and also believed that genitals were the result of Adam and Eve having grafted the halves of the forbidden fruit to their bodies. So he and his followers castrated themselves to achieve a state of purity. He also proclaimed himself the Son of God. This was a surprisingly popular and long-lasting movement, which eventually died out in the twentieth century. Another story told about Origen is that he once wanted to run into the street and proclaim himself a Christian, at a time of persecution of that faith. But his mother had hidden his clothes, and so his modesty forbade him to do it.

21. Or like those in Genesis, where Abraham prepared to sacrifice his son Isaac, to obey God, but God provided a substitute, a lamb, to take the place of the boy. This was seen as progress – man moving from human to animal sacrifice. Human sacrifice was common in pagan times. The first child was often

thought to have been fathered by a god, who would have lost some of his power to his offspring. That child would be offered up to him, as a way of returning his strength to him.

22. The fire that burnt much of Rome in AD 64 was thought to have been the result of arson. At one point it was blamed on the Emperor Nero, but (as Tacitus wrote) he focused blame on the Christian community and so commenced his persecution of them. It is said that it took his wife's intervention to prevent him from first targeting the Jews. Many others came to believe that Christians were responsible for disasters, particularly natural ones. Violence against them rose. In AD 166 a bishop was murdered in Smyrna. Eleven years later in Lyons, Christians were persecuted, arrested and put on trial. After torture, many confessed to all manner of sins. They were made to fight with wild beasts and mauled by lions.

23. Catholics have often been similarly persecuted; in Britain they were denied the right to vote from 1728 to 1793, for instance, or the right to sit in Parliament until 1829.

24. In 1260, France introduced new penalties for homosexuality. Penance was no longer sufficient; instead, after the first offence, the culprit's testicles were amputated. After the second, it was the penis, and after the third, he would be burned.

25. Fruit makes a few appearances in these stories of blame: here, in the Garden of Eden, the pomegranate seeds that Persephone ate, creating the changeable seasons. Maybe we should have been blaming fruit rather than the human or animal scapegoat all along.

26. As with Christianity, Islam was hijacked by men who interpreted the sacred texts in a way that suited them, and reduced their womenfolk in status. The Koran does not prescribe

veiling all women – only Muhammad's wives, to denote their rank.

27. If this garden was anywhere, it was in what is now southern Iraq, and formed part of the Sumerian civilization. By 5500 BC these Neolithic sites had been largely abandoned. Overgrazing by goats is thought to be one of the possible reasons.

28. The Cathars had also protested against the wealth and excesses of the Church's leadership, and sought to lead a simpler life, truer to the teachings of Christ. Orators were sent to win them round, but in vain, and a Crusade was launched on fellow Christians. The Crusaders stormed Beziers, killing 15,000 of its citizens. The soldiers asked, 'How shall we know who are the heretics?' The papal legate replied, 'Kill them all, the Lord will know his own.'

29. At this time, magic – fortune-telling, potions and charms – was widely believed in, as was sorcery, the use of supernatural means to commit harmful acts. There was plenty of overlap between this and the Christian faith so the Church sought to suppress these superstitions and replace them with its own. Priests performed exorcisms and cured ill patients and animals. This was not always a complicated matter. Say a priest was called to deal with a stricken herd of cattle. These were usually kept in such cramped conditions that sickness was inevitable, but in days of relative scientific ignorance it was assumed that the beasts were bewitched. All a successful exorcist would need to do would be to allow air in and freshen things up, and recovery would begin.

30. What starts as satire is so often reborn as propaganda, as with *The Protocols of the Elders of Zion*. Equally, what was written as allegory – i.e. much of the Bible – gets read literally, something

that should be read as poetry being treated as a legal document. But as Diarmaid MacCulloch says, 'The Bible speaks with many voices, including shouts of anger against God.' It can be interpreted in so many different ways.

31. Diarmaid MacCullough – *A History of Christianity*. John Demos says 50,000 – 100,000 in *The Enemy Within: 2,000 Years of Witch-Hunting in the Western World*.

32. Harry Lime was wrong in *The Third Man* about the dullness of the Swiss; behind the cuckoo-clock facade lurks a great capacity for violence. Five hundred suspected witches were burned in Geneva in 1515–6.

33. Charles Mackay – *Extraordinary Popular Delusions and the Madness of Crowds*, p.503–4.

34. An example of the range of victims can be seen from the trials that happened in Würzburg from 1627–9. One hundred and fifty-seven people were burned; the list included 3 actors, 4 innkeepers, 3 councilmen, 14 vicars of the cathedral, the burgomaster's lady, the apothecary's wife and daughter, two choristers and Göbel Babelin, the city's prettiest girl. Rich and poor suffered alike, and 32 vagrants were burned.

35. These confessions and the witness statements were published barely a month after the trials took place (a shock to anyone who thought that the modern age had a monopoly on grisly, voyeuristic publishing). The pamphlet sold well, needless to say, under the title, 'A true and exact Relation of the severall Informations, Examinations, and Confessions of the late Witches'.

36. There were prominent voices who denied the existence of witchcraft, notably Johann Weyer, Pietro d'Apone and Reginald Scot, in Germany, Italy and England respectively. But they were

denounced by the likes of James I for their heresy. To deny the existence of witchcraft was nothing but witchcraft itself.

37. The Scots, however, were not so frugal, and burning was their preferred method of execution.

38. There is an ancient precedent for swimming suspected witches. *The Code of Hammurabi*, from the eighteenth century BC, states that: 'If a man has put a spell upon another man and it is not justified, he upon whom the spell is laid shall go to the holy river; into the holy river shall he plunge. If the holy river overcome him and he is drowned, the man who put the spell upon him shall take possession of his house. If the holy river declares him innocent and he remains unharmed the man who laid the spell shall be put to death. He that plunged into the river shall take possession of the house of him who laid the spell upon him.' Rivers were often used as a way of ritually purifying people, but usually by washing them rather than drowning them.

39. There is some scriptural justification for this. Exodus 21:28 states: 'If an ox gore a man or a woman, that they die: then the ox shall be surely stoned, and his flesh shall not be eaten; but the owner of the ox shall be quit.'

40. In June 2010 Kerviel was put on trial for defrauding the bank he worked for. His trades lost them an unprecedented amount of money and he was accused of covering his tracks, as well as recklessness. His defence was that he did what was standard practice among his colleagues on the trading floor, that his superiors were aware of what he did, nicknaming him 'the cash machine', and that it was the bank's haste in unwinding his positions (unloading his investments) that meant so much was lost, even causing a market crash. The French financial system was ranged against him, and later that year he was sentenced to

five years in prison (with two suspended) and to repay the entire sum of his losses.

41. Mary Mallon found herself named after a disease, becoming known as Typhoid Mary. She was thought to have been the first healthy carrier of typhoid, and to have infected 47 people with the disease. She was a cook and there were outbreaks in almost every kitchen she worked in. Despite being identified by a sanitary officer as the source, she vehemently denied having typhoid and resisted all attempts to quarantine her or prevent her from working in kitchens. She died in 1969, of pneumonia.

42. Like his fellow thinker, Albert Camus, Icke played in goal, though that is perhaps the only thing they have in common. Icke was involved with the Green Party in the 1990s before resigning and beginning his 'Turquoise period' when he wore only turquoise, so as better to conduct positive energy.

43. In his excellent book on conspiracy theories, *Voodoo Histories*, David Aaronovitch points out what a relief it must have been to the Kaiser to find that he wasn't responsible for starting the First World War after all.

44. Zola had a huge reputation at the time, not just as a novelist. He had previously defended the Impressionists when the establishment was determined to deride them.

45. Sometimes we are responsible for the disasters that befall us. This is illustrated by what is called the progress trap, where we advance too much, too quickly, and perish in the process. An example of this is how man moved from killing a single mammoth at a time, to driving the whole herd over the cliff. The former is sustainable; with the latter you have destroyed your food source. The atom bomb could be described as a progress

trap, as could some forms of biological warfare. They have given man the power to destroy life on earth.

46. Although Ronald Wright points out that we are running twenty-first century software on hardware that was last upgraded 5,000 years ago.

SELECT BIBLIOGRAPHY

Aaronovitch, David – *Voodoo Histories: The Role of the Conspiracy Theory in Shaping Modern History* (Jonathan Cape, 2009)

Addison, Chris – *It Wasn't Me: Why Everybody Else Is to Blame and You're Not* (Hodder & Stoughton, 2008)

Armstrong, Karen – *A History of God* (William Heinemann, 1993)
——— *The Bible: The Biography* (Atlantic, 2007)

Barnes, Julian – *A History of the World in 10 1/2 Chapters* (Jonathan Cape, 1989)

Blond, Anthony – *A Brief History of the Private Lives of the Roman Emperors* (Robinson, 2008)

Brennan, Herbie – *Death: The Great Mystery of Life* (Carroll & Graf, 2002)

Burleigh, Michael – *The Third Reich: A New History* (Macmillan, 2000)

Buxton, Richard (Ed.) – *Oxford Readings in Greek Religion* (Oxford University Press, 2000)

Campbell, Joseph – *The Hero with a Thousand Faces* (Fontana, 1993)

Davies, Nick – *Flat Earth News* (Chatto & Windus, 2008)

Dawkins, Richard – *The God Delusion* (Transworld, 2006)

Demos, John – *The Enemy Within: 2,000 Years of Witch-Hunting in the Western World* (Viking, 2008)

Diamond, Jared – *Guns, Germs and Steel: A Short History of Everybody for the Last 13,000 Years* (Chatto & Windus, 1997)
——— *Collapse: How Societies Choose to Fail or Survive* (Allen Lane, 2005)

Diamond, John – *Snake Oil and Other Preoccupations* (Vintage, 2001)

Douglas, Tom – *Scapegoats: Transferring Blame* (Routledge, 1995)

Duff, Charles – *A Handbook on Hanging* (New York Review of Books, 2001)

Dworkin, Andrea – *Scapegoat: The Jews, Israel, and Women's Liberation* (Virago, 2000)

Ehrenreich, Barbara – *Smile or Die: How Positive Thinking Fooled America and the World* (Granta, 2009)

Elliott, J.H. and Brockliss, L.W.B. (Eds.) – *The World of the Favourite* (Yale University Press, 1999)

Evans, E.P. – *The Criminal Prosecution and Capital Punishment of Animals: The Lost History of Europe's Animal Trials* (Faber & Faber, 1987)

Fergusson, Adam – *When Money Dies: The Nightmare of the Weimar Hyper-Inflation* (Old Street Publishing, 2010)

Fischer, Steven Roger – *Island at the End of the World: The Turbulent History of Easter Island* (Reaktion Books, 2005)

Follain, John – *The Last Godfathers: The Rise and Fall of the Mafia's Most Powerful Family* (Hodder & Stoughton, 2008)

Frazer, James George – *The Golden Bough* (Oxford World's Classics, 1994)

Gaskill, Malcolm – *Witchfinders: A Seventeenth-Century English Tragedy* (John Murray, 2005)

Girard, René – *The Scapegoat* (Johns Hopkins University Press, 1985)

Graves, Robert – *The White Goddess* (Faber & Faber, 1999)

Gray, John – *Black Mass: Apocalyptic Religion and the Death of Utopia* (Allen Lane, 2007)

Green, Toby – *Inquisition: The Reign of Fear* (Macmillan, 2007)

Haswell-Smith, Hamish – *The Scottish Islands* (Canongate, 2004)

Hitchens, Christopher – *God Is Not Great: The Case Against Religion* (Atlantic Books, 2007)

Holland, Jack – *A Brief History of Misogyny: The World's Oldest Prejudice* (Robinson, 2006)

Holland, Tom – *Rubicon: The Triumph and Tragedy of the Roman Republic* (Abacus, 2003)

Jong, Erica – *Witches* (Harry N. Abrams, 1981)

Jung, Carl – *Jung: Selected Writings* (Fontana, 1983)

Kadri, Sadakat – *The Trial: A History from Socrates to O.J. Simpson* (HarperCollins, 2005)

King, Melanie – *The Dying Game: A Curious History of Death* (Oneworld, 2008)

Klein, Melanie – *The Psycho-Analysis of Children* (Vintage, 1997)

Lanchester, John – *Whoops! Why Everyone Owes Everyone and No One Can Pay* (Penguin, 2010)

Laughland, John – *A History of Political Trials: From Charles I to Saddam Hussein* (Peter Lang, 2008)

Leach, Maria (Ed.) – *Funk and Wagnall's Standard Dictionary of Folklore, Mythology and Legend* (HarperCollins, 1984)

MacCulloch, Diarmaid – *A History of Christianity* (Allen Lane, 2009)

Mackay, Charles – *Extraordinary Popular Delusions and the Madness of Crowds* (Three Rivers Press, 1980)

Mackay, Christopher S. (Trans.) – *The Hammer of the Witches: A Complete Translation of the Malleus Maleficarum* (Cambridge University Press, 2009)

McConnachie, James and Tudge, Robin – *The Rough Guide to Conspiracy Theories* (Rough Guides, 2005)

McNeil, Donald J. – 'Finding a Scapegoat When Epidemics Strike' (*New York Times*, 31.8.09)

Moynahan, Brian – *William Tyndale: If God Spare My Life* (Abacus, 2002)

Parker, Robert – *Athenian Religion: A History* (Oxford University Press, 1997)

Perera, Sylvia Brinton – *The Scapegoat Complex: Toward a Mythology of Shadow and Guilt*, (Inner City Books, 1985)

Peter, Laurence J. and Hull, Raymond – *The Peter Principle: Why Things Always Go Wrong* (Souvenir Press, 1969)

Reinhart, Carmen M. & Rogoff, Kenneth S. – *This Time Is Different: Eight Centuries of Financial Folly* (Princeton University Press, 2009)

Renault, Mary – *The Praise Singer* (Arrow, 2004)

Ronson, Jon – *Them: Adventures with Extremists* (Picador, 2001)

Service, Robert – *The Penguin History of Modern Russia: From Tsarism to the Twenty-First Century* (Allen Lane, 1997)

Showalter, Elaine – *Hystories: Hysterical Epidemics and Modern Culture* (Picador, 1997)

Stanford, Peter – *The Devil: A Biography* (William Heinemann, 1996)

Steel, Tom – *The Life and Death of St Kilda: The Moving Story of a Vanished Island Community* (Fontana, 1975)

Sutherland, Stuart – *Irrationality* (Pinter & Martin, 2007)

Tavris, Carol and Aronson, Elliot – *Mistakes Were Made (But Not by Me): Why We Justify Foolish Beliefs, Bad Decisions and Hurtful Acts* (Pinter & Martin, 2008)

Thompson, Damian – *Counterknowledge: How We Surrendered to Conspiracy Theories, Quack Medicine, Bogus Science and Fake History* (Atlantic Books, 2008)

Tuchman, Barbara W. – *The March of Folly: From Troy to Vietnam* (Abacus, 1990)

Wheen, Francis – *Hoo-Hahs and Passing Frenzies* (Atlantic Books, 2002)

——— *How Mumbo-Jumbo Conquered the World: A Short History of Modern Delusions* (Fourth Estate, 2004)

Wright, Ronald – *A Short History of Progress* (Canongate, 2005)

Zeldin, Theodore – *An Intimate History of Humanity* (Vintage, 1998)

Zinn, Howard – *The Twentieth Century: A People's History* (HarperPerennial, 2008)

ACKNOWLEDGEMENTS

I would like to thank my family, most of all my parents; my agent Nicola Barr for her tireless work, along with Hellie Ogden, Chris Wellbelove and Claudia Young; and everyone at Duckworth and the Overlook Press, in particular Jon Jackson, Suzannah Rich, Tracy Carns and Peter Mayer.

I would also like to thank the following for their ideas, encouragement and support at various points in the writing of this book: Lisa Baker, Lowdy Brabyn, Tom Bromley, Alex Burghart, Helen Coyle, Hermione Eyre, Thomas Hodgkinson, Louisa Joyner, Thomas Mogford, Mary Morris, Maggie Phillips, Damian Pitman, Henry Porter, Rebecca Rose, Charlie Smith, Laura Susijn and Roly Walter.

★